apartment therapy presents

real **homes**
real **people**
hundreds of real
design solutions

apartment

Maxwell Gillingham-Ryan

WITH JILL SLATER AND JANEL LABAN

therapy presents

Real Homes. Real People. Hundreds of Real Design Solutions.

CHRONICLE BOOKS

SAN FRANCISCO

Manufactured in China
Designed by Lucinda Hitchcock
Typefaces: Chaparral, Helvetica
Focus, Snell Roundhand, and
Bickham Script

10 9 8 7 6 5 4 3 2 1

Chronicle Books LLC
680 Second Street
San Francisco, California 94107
www.chroniclebooks.com

LIBRARY OF CONGRESS
CATALOGING-IN-PUBLICATION
DATA
Gillingham-Ryan, Maxwell.
Apartment Therapy presents real
homes, real people, hundreds of
real design solutions /
Maxwell Gillingham-Ryan with
Jill Slater and Janel Laban.
        p.   cm.
Includes index.
ISBN-13: 978-0-8118-5982-0
ISBN-10: 0-8118-5982-7
1. Apartment Therapy (Firm)
2. Interior decoration — United
States. 3. Apartments — United
States. I. Slater, Jill. II. Laban,
Janel. III. Title.

NK2004.3.A63A4 2008
747 — DC22
2007017179

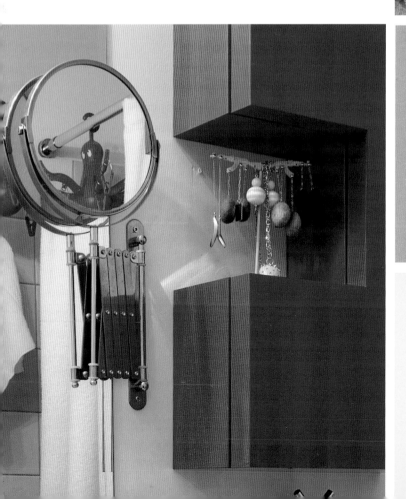

PLEASE NOTE: The experiences of the homeowners featured in this book varied from project to project. Should you attempt to imitate their design prowess (which you should!), please expect to encounter situations that are not covered in this book. Be careful when using materials that may be toxic, and always defer to the manufacturer's product instructions when painting, building, or crafting. Chronicle Books, the author, and the homeowners featured in this book hereby disclaim any and all liability resulting from injuries or damages caused by imitating the ideas described herein.

contents

introduction

"NOTHING YOU DO FOR YOUR HOME IS EVER WASTED."

This is the Apartment Therapy mantra.

In my work as a teacher and interior designer over nearly fifteen years, I've seen that the importance of the home in our lives has only increased. I used to think of home as the place where we cook, eat, and sleep. I now understand it as a force that shapes our daily lives. More than just a physical shelter, the home is both a second skin that protects us from the world outside and an emotional center that nourishes us and supports our innermost dreams.

Whether you live in a rental apartment in New York City or own a house in Seattle, your home is the one space on earth that you can call your own. You owe it to yourself to make it as beautiful, organized, and healthy as you can.

By taking care of your home, you are taking care of yourself. A healthy home will nurture and support you. Although professional psychotherapy can take years to bring about change, improving your home has an instant therapeutic effect. No matter how big or small, the changes make a resounding difference in the way you think and feel about yourself.

I started Apartment Therapy in 2001 as an interior design service. Back then I helped people in New York City transform their homes. Arriving at their doorsteps with open ears, design advice, and a box of tools on the back of my scooter, I listened to why people didn't love their homes and then did whatever I could to make them happy. I worked with them to throw out what they didn't need, and then bought furniture, hung curtains, painted, and even washed windows. I didn't have a business plan, an office, or even a cell phone. Falling back on a year of savings and trusting the hunch that many New Yorkers wanted design help and didn't know where to turn, I started my company.

Over the years, I have visited hundreds of homes, and Apartment Therapy has grown from a one-man operation into a design and media company devoted to listening to people and connecting them with the resources and information they need.

At its essence, Apartment Therapy offers real design solutions for real people. High-end interior designers are inaccessible to the average person, and television makeover shows whet the appetite but are unrealistic in their reliance on teams of carpenters

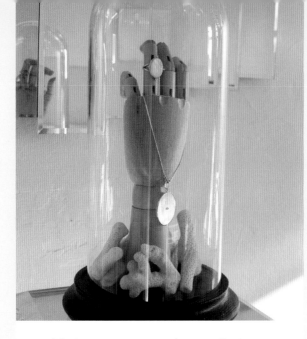

and designers to turn around a space. Design magazines are also a tease. Most are not about comfort or beauty, but about showing off expensive design statements that often have little relation to the people who live in the homes. Most of us benefit not from seeing how celebrities and the ultra-wealthy live, but from seeing how real people create real homes.

When Apartment Therapy went online as a daily blog in 2004, I was able to realize my dream of sharing my clients' homes. I knew that these modest yet beautiful spaces with their great ideas and creative solutions would inspire others. Our online House Tours, accomplished by a simple upload to our Web site, use slide shows and interviews to take readers of the blog through the homes. Now, thousands of people can easily visit and see what others have done.

This book takes three years' worth of House Tours from the Apartment Therapy blogs and puts them in one volume. Each home is intended to inspire in different ways. Whether owned or rented, the homes run the gamut from roomy to tiny, modern to traditional. They come from east, west, north, and south, and feature people who spent pennies and those who broke the bank. Although many people in the book are involved in design and the arts, only a few are interior designers by profession and none of the rest hired a professional interior decorator to make creative decisions for them. What they all share is a passion for improving their surroundings and for creating homes that make them smile every time they come in the door.

The Apartment Therapy community is primarily an online community, so this is a rare opportunity to show you all of these homes, and provide you with invaluable resources, in a single volume.

HOW
THIS BOOK
WORKS

Each chapter has four distinct parts. The first part introduces you to the home dweller and gives an overview of the home and why we think it's so great. The second part is a survey filled out by each subject that reveals his or her personal thoughts, inspiration, challenges, and advice. The third part takes you on a visual tour of the home and includes a floor plan.

Whenever possible, we provide sources for the furniture, fixtures, and materials used. At the end of the chapter, you'll find contact information for all the sources.

I HOPE THAT YOU PUT ALL THE STORIES AND IDEAS HERE TO GOOD USE. THESE ARE REAL HOMES CREATED BY REAL PEOPLE—AND EACH IS EXTRAORDINARY IN ITS OWN WAY.

MAXWELL GILLINGHAM-RYAN

photos by
mike
butler

01.

alison's design
to the max

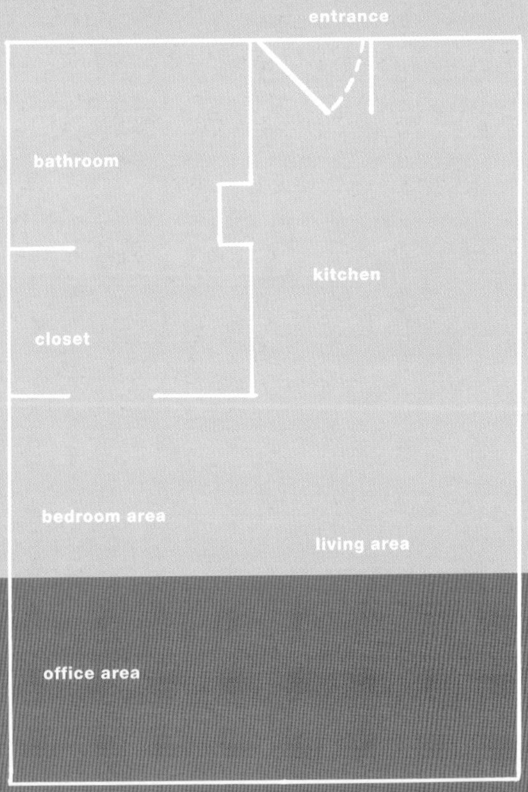

NAME: ALISON BRUNGART

PROFESSION: FURNITURE AND INTERIORS DESIGNER

LOCATION: SOUTH BEACH, FLORIDA

OWNED/RENTED: OWNED

SIZE: 396 SQUARE FEET

TYPE: STUDIO IN A 1970s APARTMENT BUILDING

YEARS LIVED IN: 2.5

entrance

bathroom

closet

kitchen

bedroom area

living area

office area

ALISON HAS APPLIED EVERYTHING SHE KNOWS TO MAKE THIS SPACE SUPERFUNCTIONAL.

She removed two non-load-bearing walls, built custom closets, and efficiently planned every inch of floor space.

Aside from the intelligent use of space, what struck us first was that Alison's home is very modern and minimal, yet not cold. Her feminine style softens the sharp edges and straight lines, and her smart use of color warms up the woodwork. The impressionistic artwork invites your eyes to pause before moving on. There is something about the green bedspread contrasted with the pink slippers on the floor that we find entrancing. When a space is minimal in design, every personal detail informs the decor.

Alison's use of shelving as a room divider works beautifully. The unit aligns with the living room wall, making a natural boundary between bedroom and living room. Because some of the shelves are open and airy, the large piece doesn't seem massive. She chose similar woodwork for most of her furniture so pieces like the room divider and bed are consistent, even though they were built at different times. The uniform use of light wood avoids visual clutter and makes the space seem bright and open.

Alison's home is compact. The 396 square feet comfortably accommodate her living room, dining area, kitchen, office, and bedroom.

What Friends Say

They say that it's cozy and comfortable. Organized and always clean. I don't have the luxury of space to be messy!

Biggest Embarrassment

Honestly, I don't really have one. Because it is such a small space, everything is exposed. After I worked so hard to make it perfect for me, I won't let there be anything embarrassing!

Proudest DIY

I created a beautiful space, with a challenging size, on a very small budget. I'm proud because it's a project I did with only myself in mind.

Biggest Indulgence

Design Within Reach red sliding sofa. A splurge, but worth every penny.

Best Advice

It's your home — design it for you!

alison's
survey

Style

I'm not afraid of color, but still want to create an overall clean and cozy look that's modern. My style is retro-funky yet functional.

Inspiration

The beach, nature, the South Beach flavor.

Favorite Element

The room divider. It's a piece that I designed for the space. It looks great and gives me privacy as well as storage!

Biggest Challenge

Space, storage, and keeping all of my favorite things without being cluttered. Also, I wanted to use all the pieces I designed and fabricated in college, so I had to make sure my overall design would incorporate them.

Alison designed the room divider. It replaced a wall that once delineated a separate bedroom. The TV rotates so it can be seen from the bed. She also designed the bar, then built it herself using Baltic birch plywood, purpleheart veneer, aluminum, and glass. The Bellini chair is from Design Within Reach and is one of a pair. The painting above the bar is by Reed Smith.

Dream Source

I have always collected things. In high school, it started with my green pottery and vintage fans. I'm always looking for pieces with character. I love new designs but can only usually afford a piece at a time, which makes each thing I own very special.

The mirror was once a sliding door for a closet. Alison collected the old fans from thrift stores over the years.

when a space is minimal in design, every personal detail informs the decor.

(above) Alison designed the built-in shelving below the windows and the bed with storage underneath. The **Saarinen Tulip** side table is from **Knoll**, as is the **Marcel Breuer Laccio** table. The red sliding sofa from **Design Within Reach** has a **Maharam** pillow. While in art school, Alison built and designed the postcard cabinet and clock on the shelves. **Flor** modular carpet tiles in Surf and Midnight Blue from their **Solid Foundation** collection cover the floor. The blue contributes to the soothing tones used throughout the apartment.

The wall cabinets (left) hide the air-conditioning system and provide storage. The **George Nelson** clock is from **Design Within Reach**. Alison designed and built the green chair using **Corian** and stainless steel, and painted the work that hangs above the bed (far left).

Alison made only a few changes to the
original kitchen. She moved an undercounter
refrigerator into the pantry and replaced
it with a new cabinet. The Aero counter stools
are from Design Within Reach. Alison's
Fiestaware collection has grown steadily
since high school.

In the bedroom (opposite), the wall cabinets extending from the living room become a desk that takes advantage of the natural light. The closet/dressing area is also a connector hallway between the bedroom and the kitchen. It contains a built-in dresser and floor-to-ceiling maple plywood shelving. The furniture is made from medium-density fiberboard (MDF) with a maple veneer. The legs are from stock aluminum cut to fit. Alison wanted the furniture raised off the floor so it would appear to be floating. Architectural blackout shades with a screen in front of them block the light when Alison wants to sleep in.

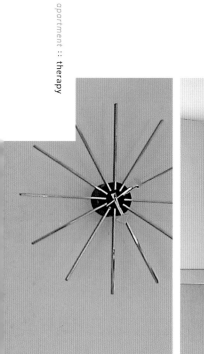

It's
your
home—
design it
for you!

RESOURCES

DESIGN WITHIN REACH: dwr.com

FLOR: florcatalog.com

KNOLL: knoll.com

photos by
jill
slater

alton and andré's deco light in chelsea

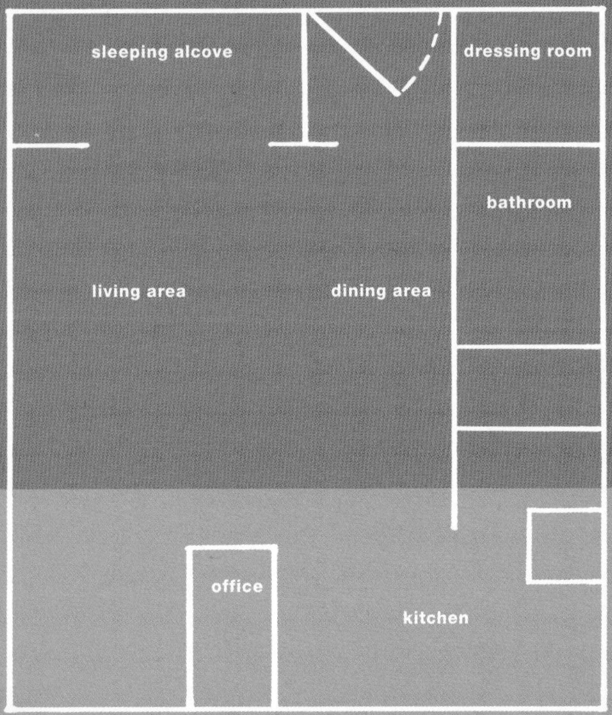

NAME: ALTON DULANEY
AND ANDRÉ DA COSTA
PROFESSION: JEWELRY DESIGNERS
LOCATION: CHELSEA, NYC
OWNED/RENTED: RENTED
SIZE: 485 SQUARE FEET
TYPE: STUDIO IN LONDON
TERRACE TOWERS (1930s
HIGH-RISE)
YEARS LIVED IN: 2

sleeping alcove

dressing room

bathroom

living area

dining area

office

kitchen

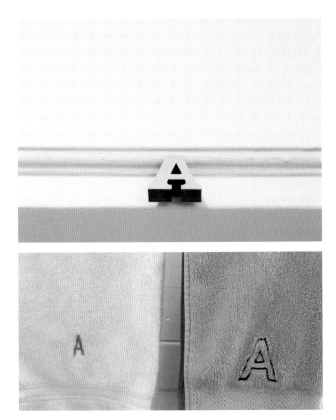

Two things immediately caught our attention:

the bold mix of dissimilar furniture styles and the beautiful paint job that highlights the prewar walls and molding.

Alton and André's style is modern eclectic. Their coffee table and two side chairs are Danish modern. Their lighting fixtures are from the 1970s. The stars of the show, and the pieces that set the tone, are the 1950s faux Victorian sofa and armchair from a flea market.

We remember spotting lots of this stuff in antique stores and yard sales in years past, and since seeing the pieces at Alton and André's, we've noticed this updated traditional, ornate style popping up in hot shops like Jonathan Adler, Moss, and Brocade Home (which bases its entire look on the style). Alton and André prove that it pays to turn to the past to find your way forward again.

Prewar buildings in NYC have great bones: wide rooms, beefy molding, and thick plaster walls. There is so much character in these apartments already that there's no point fighting it and trying to go too modern. Alton and André have done a great job highlighting the original detailing and emphasizing the square shape of the rooms through their choice of furniture.

As you look around, don't miss the bedroom. It's hidden away behind the doors of what looks like a closet.

Talk about lucky! Alton and André have homes in New York, Texas, and Rio de Janeiro and use their Chelsea apartment as a pied-à-terre. They don't need to squeeze in a ton of belongings or fit in a lot of functions. The apartment can be just the way they want it: a compact, cheerful residence that reflects their edgy approach to decor.

(left) For a Manhattan apartment, this is a huge walk-in closet. It holds Alton and André's entire wardrobe, as well as an industrial steamer, and serves as a dressing room. "We are fashionistas," Alton says. They found the mid-twentieth-century chest of drawers at the Hell's Kitchen Flea Market. *The art deco mirrors and wooden heads are from* Mantiques Modern.

(opposite, top) Alton and André found the George Nelson *bench at a Chelsea design store and the black wooden obelisks at* Mantiques Modern. *The area rug is by* Merida *from* ABC Carpet & Home. *The couch, chair, and side table came from the* Hell's Kitchen Flea Market. *They kept the original plastic upholstery, which was in perfect condition, and painted the brown wood white. The specially commissioned* Kysa Johnson *paintings depict the molecular structures of gold, diamond, and platinum, reflecting Alton and André's jewelry design. A black Polish glass vase from* Crate & Barrel *sits on a wood-grain pedestal from* Stereoluz, *which is lit from within. The lamp is a house-warming gift from a neighbor.*

alton and andré's
survey

Style:

Modern masculine glamour.

Inspiration:

A combination of airiness and solidity, to showcase our aesthetic lifestyle—for entertaining friends and clients.

Favorite Element:

The variety of ambiences, all in less than 500 square feet.

Biggest Challenge:

Achieving maximum effect in minimum space.

What Friends Say:

Perfectly curated yet ideal for socializing.

Biggest Embarrassment:

Window A/C unit.

Proudest DIY:

Customized bed elevated to create additional storage space.

Biggest Indulgence:

An original Kysa Johnson artwork.

Best Advice:

Choose a theme and run with it, and "a place for everything and everything in its place" (Reverend C. A. Goodrich, 1827).

Dream Sources:

Flea markets around the world, Design Within Reach, PlexiCraft.

*Alton & André
kept the original
1930s deco bathroom
as they found it.
The built-in, fold-out
scale is an original
feature.*

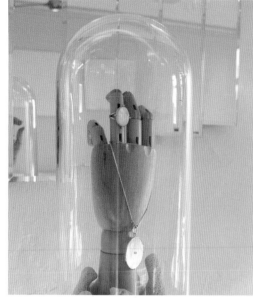

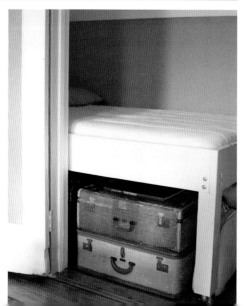

(left, middle) André and Alton love the apartment's southern exposure. They bought the miniature ponytail bonsai at the **Flower District** *in Manhattan and put them in Indian pewter pots.*

(right, middle) The efficient home office consists of a Danish modern desk from the **Hell's Kitchen Flea Market** *and a Lucite pilot's chair with chrome base, which was a gift.*

(left, bottom) The custom bed on wheels, by **Greg Wildes,** *fits the tight space of the sleeping alcove and is extra high to provide storage.*

(above, and opposite, top left) *The apartment's color scheme, like Alton and André's wardrobe, is a limited palette of black, white, gray, brown, silver, and gold. On the walls they used Calm Air, Subtle Silver, and Shadow Black by* **Behr** *at* **Home Depot**. *The glass domes throughout the apartment are from* **Mantiques Modern**. *The jewelry display is by* **A. COSTA de luxe**.

(opposite, top right) *Each apartment in the building has a bedroom with two French doors. The space is just large enough, forty-eight inches wide, to hold an antique full-sized bed. The headboard is from the* **Design Compendium**. *The hanging lamp is a glass tube from a vintage chandelier.*

RESOURCES

A. COSTA DE LUXE: acostadeluxe.com

ABC CARPET & HOME: abchome.com

BEHR: behr.com

CRATE & BARREL: crateandbarrel.com

DESIGN COMPENDIUM: design-compendium.com

FLOWER DISTRICT: 28th Street between Broadway and 7th Avenue

HELL'S KITCHEN FLEA MARKET: hellskitchenfleamarket.com

HOME DEPOT: homedepot.com

MANTIQUES MODERN: mantiquesmodern.1stdibs.com

PLEXICRAFT: plexicraft.com

STEREOLUZ: stereoluz.net

03.
andreas's greektown loft

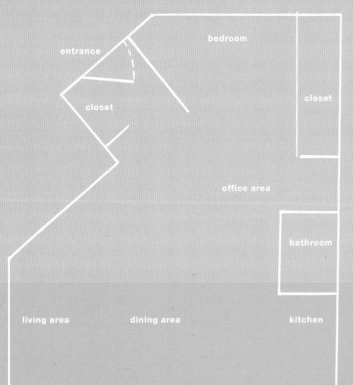

entrance

bedroom

closet

closet

office area

bathroom

living area   dining area   kitchen

NAME: ANDREAS LARSSON
PROFESSION: PHOTOGRAPHER
LOCATION: GREEKTOWN, CHICAGO
OWNED/RENTED: OWNED
SIZE: 1,100 SQUARE FEET
TYPE: LOFT IN A LATE-1800s INDUSTRIAL BUILDING
YEARS LIVED IN: 1

IF MINIMALISM IS YOUR STYLE, YOU'LL LIKE THE STORY OF

Andreas's wonderful loft. He took a traditionally decorated multiroom space with exposed wood beams, removed the interior walls and dividers, painted the walls and ceiling white and the floors deep black, and then filled the stripped-down loft with a selection of beautiful things.

The furniture sits low to the floor, and many pieces are vintage midcentury modern. Sunlight fills the entire space.

The loft, which is like a large studio, looks as if a Calvin Klein ad is about to be shot. What is most interesting about Andreas's project is that although his apartment looks high-end, many of the furnishings come from IKEA, eBay, and several midcentury modern shops.

We particularly like that Andreas chose IKEA kitchen cabinets for living room storage. The standard Akurum cabinets are attached low on the wall, creating elegant storage for a fraction of the cost of custom cabinetry. Because the cabinets are modular and come in a variety of finishes, this solution would

suit almost any space. We've heard of many uses for IKEA kitchen materials, but this is by far one of the best.

Andreas's choice of midcentury pieces gives what might otherwise be an antiseptic environment a strong character and a cozy, lived-in feeling. The oversized Florence Knoll desk and beefy Eames executive chair look inviting. Similarly, the vintage-style octagonal tile in the kitchen and entryway gives these areas a slight retro quality.

Andreas proves that it's all about balance. If you want clean, white, and minimal, it helps to throw in some old, grainy, or rich texture so that you don't feel as if you're living in a laboratory.

andreas's
survey

Style

This is a tricky one. I guess clean, simple, Danish, American, Italian, midcentury modern with some newer elements.

Inspiration

A space that is clean and uncluttered without seeming empty. A space where I can enjoy the spaciousness while feeling comfortable and very much at home.

Favorite Element

One of my favorite elements is how, no matter where you sit, you can see everything and get different perspectives.

Biggest Challenge

Finding a balance between a comfortable home environment and a functional work setting that is organized and not an eyesore.

What Friends Say

Everyone has a reaction. To me, that is the biggest compliment because it means I have done something different and reflective of myself.

Biggest Embarrassment

I am not embarrassed about anything — well, maybe the dirty laundry in my bathroom!

Proudest DIY

Installing the industrial garage doors on my closets. It gives off a kind of a rustic vibe, while still looking very modern and innovative.

Biggest Indulgence

The time and money I spend tracking down designer furniture. While not necessary, I love it and feel that I just have to have it when I find it.

Best Advice

Don't take too much advice and buy only what you really want. If you can afford only one great thing per year, you'll be happier in the long run.

Dream Source

Dansk Møbelkunst.

The living area has lots of hidden storage.

*The big, comfortable Havana sofa from **Design Within Reach** (top) has storage under the seat where, Andreas says, "you can hide half the apartment." Additional storage is in the long stretch of **IKEA** cabinets along the wall. To round out the seating area, he hunted down the vintage **Arne Jacobsen** table and **Eames** rocker. Andreas has no television – instead, he uses a projector hooked up to his cable box and DVD player, which displays directly onto the wall. Andreas searched a long time for the **Florence Knoll** credenza before finding it on **eBay**. It holds an early-production **Arne Jacobsen** bar set (opposite, top left), which Andreas collected piece by piece. The glass sculpture (opposite, top right) by Chicago artist **Pearl Dick** was Andreas's first art auction purchase.*

*For the hanging wall storage (above, bottom), Andreas chose **IKEA Akurum** kitchen cabinets. The simple lines suit the modern furnishings. The cabinets hide the speakers when not in use. The vase is from **Sprout Home**.*

*A **Sapien** bookshelf (opposite, bottom) from **Design Within Reach** stores lots of reading material in a small footprint.*

(above, top left) Andreas bought the **Super Elliptical**
table from **Retromodern** *and surrounded it with Ant*
chairs by **Arne Jacobsen**. *He constructed the hanging*
lights with parts from **Bright Electrical Supply**. *Vintage-*
style octagonal ceramic tiles from **Tile Outlet** *were*
installed on the kitchen floor and in the entryway.

The loft's walls and ceilings were painted with **Benjamin**
Moore *Egg White, and the hardwood floors with glossy*
porch paint with no primer. The office, closet, bathroom,
and bedroom are on a raised platform, an original feature
of the loft intended to reduce the sound between units.

(opposite, top right) The oversized desk by Florence Knoll *(a piece that everyone loves, Andreas says) pairs beautifully with the vintage* Eames *Time-Life task chair from* Converso Modern.

(opposite, bottom left) The closet door – the DIY project that Andreas is most proud of – is an industrial door from Steel Building. *The vintage* Eames *side chair is second production. He found the* Eames *coat rack at* Circa 50.

(opposite, bottom right) The large curtain on tracks, from IKEA, *hides storage. Andreas made the light fixture with materials from* Bright Electrical Supply. *The* Eames *side table comes from* Circa 50, *and the* Knoll *bed from* Collage Classics.

RESOURCES

BENJAMIN MOORE: benjaminmoore.com
BRIGHT ELECTRICAL SUPPLY: brightelectric.com
CIRCA 50: circa50.com
COLLAGE CLASSICS: collageclassics.com
CONVERSO MODERN: conversomod.com
DESIGN WITHIN REACH: dwr.com
EBAY: ebay.com
FLORENCE KNOLL: knoll.com
IKEA: ikea.com
PEARL DICK: pearldick.com
RETROMODERN: retromodern.com
SPROUT HOME: store.sprouthome.com
STEEL BUILDING: steelbuilding.com
TILE OUTLET: 773.276.2662

photos by
jill
slater

04.
bri and chad's
fab on a budget

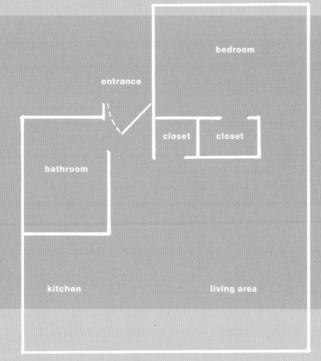

bedroom

entrance

closet   closet

bathroom

kitchen   living area

NAME: BRI AND CHAD
PROFESSION: ILLUSTRATOR AND
MASTER'S CANDIDATE (BRI)
AND ART HISTORY STUDENT (CHAD)
LOCATION: CHELSEA, NYC
OWNED/RENTED: RENTED
SIZE: 350 SQUARE FEET
TYPE: 1-BEDROOM IN 4-STORY
WALK-UP BUILT IN THE
EARLY 1970s
YEARS LIVED IN: 1

Bri and Chad stunned us
with their playful, chic style
they call "fooly"—their homegrown
mix of modern, classic, and
kitsch elements.

Clearly beyond their years in interior design ability, they have created what one friend calls "a grown-up apartment" while living on the strictest of diets: the student budget. Despite this limitation, they aimed for more than putting together a purely functional space. To do this, they scavenged family attics, sharpened their sewing skills, and found creative DIY solutions for many of their problems.

With a budget of only $1,000, Bri and Chad looked to sources other than retail. They started by resuscitating garage-stored family furniture. Then, to add pizzazz, they made the most with the least by being adventurous with color and pattern. The discount fabric store and the paint store became frequent stops, enabling them to realize their vision (along with an assist from Bri's mom, who helped Bri make a duvet cover and reupholster the couch). They sewed the curtains on their own.

Bri and Chad highlighted pieces of senti-mental value. They show that if something is meaningful to you and treated with reverence, other people will recognize its value and transfer its importance to the surrounding space.

Bri and Chad say their home is still a work in progress, and that "good design is always in flux."

Books and chairs dominate as design features in the small apartment. Chad found this Chinese elementary school chair at Bloom. The rooster belonged to Bri's late grandmother. Although it takes up countertop real estate in the small kitchen, she finds it comforting to have a few things around the house that remind her of the good times she and her grandmother shared.

bri and chad's
survey

Style

We call it "fooly": it's very colorful, with a combination of modern and classic lines, plus a bit of kitsch.

Inspiration

We were inspired by disparate sources, including Scandinavian design, our Oklahoma upbringings, and our shared love of art.

Favorite Element

Hands down, the bedroom.

Biggest Challenge

Our budget.

What Friends Say

When my friend Eloise first saw our place, she said, "Oh my gosh! You have a grown-up apartment!" It is one of the best things she could have said.

Biggest Embarrassment

This would have to be our bathroom. It's the one room we haven't gotten to, and it needs a lot of work.

Proudest DIY

Definitely the Post-It wall.

Biggest Indulgence

Artwork. After moving to the city, we slowly began collecting. Our favorite piece is by Brad Brown, and it cost more than everything in the apartment put together.

Best Advice

Be fearless. If you can figure out what you like, just go for it. It doesn't matter if it's conventional or avant-garde. If it's "you," that's what's really important.

Dream Source

ABC Carpet & Home is sadly out of our price range, but we love their eclectic mix and one-of-a-kind pieces.

Bri and Chad reupholstered the couch with the help of Bri's mom. The coffee table cubes are from **West Elm**. *The walls are Janovic's Excalibur Gray.*

To create a headboard (top), Bri and Chad scanned, enlarged, and cut out a photo of a Biedermeier design. They were disappointed with the black-and-white print, so they turned it over to show off the back side against the striped wall.

The table (left), located right by the door, is the official landing strip for keys, iPod, and phone (in the white bowl). Bri and Chad rescued the table from NYC's trash piles and spruced it up with **Janovic's Forest Moss** in high-gloss enamel.

Bri and Chad used red to unify
and bring personality to their
bland rental kitchen. The color
theme began with a set of inherited
cookware. They painted the rear
kitchen wall Benjamin Moore's
Lemon Freeze. The Tozai vases,
plates, and candles are from Bloom
in Newark, Delaware; the plates
on the wall are from MXYPLYZYK,
and the kitchen trays and other
accessories from Three Tarts in
Manhattan. Bri's photographs of
vegetables on the far wall are in
frames purchased at Utrecht Art
Supplies.

good design is always in flux.

Vertical stripes, in Mountain Lane
and Bird's Egg by Benjamin Moore,
give the bedroom a sophisticated look
and visually open up the space. The
floating shelves take advantage of
once-dead space above the radiator.
This red chair is from IKEA.

After a failed attempt to cover a living room wall with spray-starched torn paper, Chad had the idea of using Post-It *notes to create an interesting texture. A thousand* Post-Its *and more than a half-year later, the resilient little yellow stickies are still in place. The computer console table from* Crate & Barrel Outlet *is matched with a chair from* IKEA. *The large vase is from* West Elm.

RESOURCES

BENJAMIN MOORE: benjaminmoore.com

BLOOM: bloomfolly.com

CRATE & BARREL: crateandbarrel.com

IKEA: ikea.com

JANOVIC: janovic.com

MXYPLYZYK: mxyplyzyk.com

THREE TARTS: 3tarts.com

UTRECHT: utrechtart.com

WEST ELM: westelm.com

photos by
jill
slater

05.

charles and julie's perfect garden apartment

NAME: CHARLES AND JULIE

PROFESSION: DESIGN FIRM OWNER (CHARLES) AND ENVIRONMENTAL FUND-RAISER (JULIE)

LOCATION: UPPER EAST SIDE, NYC

OWNED/RENTED: OWNED

SIZE: 1,200 SQUARE FEET

TYPE: 1-BEDROOM IN EARLY-20th-CENTURY 4-STORY BROWNSTONE

YEARS LIVED IN: 3

We've known Charles since grade school and can honestly say that not only does he have a knack for making beautiful, cozy homes,

but his style hasn't changed one bit since we were ten years old. He grew up in a large, rambling apartment in Manhattan, surrounded by antique furniture, original artwork, and dozens of interesting personal objects. He re-created the warmth and sense of history in a long string of rentals before buying this lovely ground-floor apartment where he lives with his wife, Julie, and their young son.

You'll notice that the furniture is very eclectic, everything looks antique, and there is a tremendous amount of artwork. This eclecticism gives the home its liveliness. Very little about Charles's taste seems modern. The many traditional pieces are rarely matched and vary widely from Shaker side chairs to a Ralph Lauren loveseat to a Balinese teak bed. They work well together because they fit his aesthetic preference for well-crafted wood and stripped-down design, best exemplified in the Shaker furniture. Charles does not like frivolous decoration or filigree, and every piece hews to this view.

The framing effectively sets off the artwork. Charles has more original art than most people, and he has chosen similarly styled frames so that the different objects work together and don't clutter up the walls.

Charles's apartment successfully argues in favor of investing in good furniture and holding on to it. It contains barely a piece of "carbohydrate" filler from IKEA, Pottery Barn, or Crate & Barrel. His careful purchases cost him more, but will last forever. His furniture is all "protein"—a nourishing collection that will satisfy and endure over time.

charles and julie's
survey

Style

Japanese- and Shaker-influenced.
Comfortable. Generally organic color palette.
Warm earth tones, not too tidy . . .

Inspiration

We set out to create a serene space to
raise a very young child, to grow a garden,
to entertain when possible and read.

Favorite Element

The kitchen opening onto a garden.

Biggest Challenge

Our son George's room, or sleeping nook . . .
Taking and dedicating the space actually
improved the feel of the apartment.

What Friends Say

Transporting; welcoming; a quiet, private
respite.

Biggest Embarrassment

The bathrooms are quite small; think first
class on a Greyhound bus.

Proudest DIY

George's strange and perfect little roomlet.

Biggest Indulgence

A large, raised, clear cedar deck. We
were right to guess that the green, shady
space would always beckon.

Best Advice

Buy Le Creuset.

Dream Source

Store in Milan—G. Lorenzi—completely
out-of-reach cool stuff—modern artifacts.

A nourishing collection that will satisfy and endure over time.

*The living room rug is from **ABC Carpet & Home Warehouse**. The rocking chair on the right is a No. 7 Shaker chair from Enfield, New Hampshire. It was designed as a nursing chair and is therefore wider than most Shaker chairs. The framed print is a calligraphic work from the 1950s by Manchurian artist **Shinoda Toko**. Charles's father purchased it in Japan in the 1960s.*

Charles purchased the down couch in SoHo more than fifteen years ago. The coffee table, made of planks from an old farmhouse, was purchased in 1992 at the now-closed Portico *in SoHo. It is the perfect height for Charles's son George when he sits in his No. 1 child's Shaker chair from the 1890s. Charles inherited the side chair from his father and had it reupholstered by* Mr. Galleano *in the Bronx. The leather armchair is from* Elliott Galleries. *To create a bedroom for George, Charles carved space out of what was once a very large living room. The bedroom is behind the bookshelves.*

The top shelf of the living room unit holds a fire truck from Elliott Galleries *and a West African bike made of rubber and cans from an import store in SoHo.*

The wooden shelf that runs around the cooking and dining area holds Charles and Julie's glass vases and other objects. The wood planters are from Sammy's. *The 1850s Indian alabaster horses are from* Castano Lartigue.

The inlaid desk in the living room belonged to Charles's grandparents. The 1920s painted chair is mock bamboo. Charles had the shade custom-made at the Oriental Lamp Shade Company.

The antique Japanese bench was purchased at an antique store in Tribeca. Charles sees the bent spindles that form the back as combining Shaker design and Asian decorative style. The nineteenth-century marquetry secretary came from a Chelsea antique store. The 1920s French lamp and the pounded brass stool are from Elliott Galleries. The painting is by Becky Yazdan.

(opposite, top) The dining table, a wedding present, was made by a carpenter friend, Henry Kirchdorfer. Charles had the chairs custom built by Glenn Carlson, a master chair maker at Hancock Shaker Village. He wanted slightly wider versions of a classic Shaker design using tiger maple. The pillows on the bench are from Restoration Hardware.

(opposite, bottom left) The fireplace mantel in the living room holds two paintings of Korean vases. The restored 1908 painting is by an American Impressionist painter who was friends with Charles's grandfather.

(opposite, bottom right) The wonderful Victorian-era chair once belonged to Charles's great-grandmother. The painting is by Becky Yazdan.

(above) The floor is covered with twelve-inch terra-cotta tiles. Charles designed a raised deck for the rear yard. Many of the black-and-white photographs came from Alan Klotz Gallery.

RESOURCES

ABC CARPET & HOME: abchome.com

ALAN KLOTZ GALLERY: photocollect.com

ELLIOTT GALLERIES: 155 East Seventy-ninth Street, 212.861.2222

HANCOCK SHAKER VILLAGE: hancockshakervillage.org

ORIENTAL LAMP SHADE CO.: orientallampshade.com

RESTORATION HARDWARE: restorationhardware.com

SAMMY'S: 484 Broome Street, 212.343.2357

BECKY YAZDAN: beckyyazdan.com

photos by
**jill
slater**

06.
curtis's paint
by numbers

entrance

closet

closet

closet

bedroom area

dining room

living area | kitchen | bathroom

NAME: CURTIS ROBERTSON
PROFESSION: ARTIST
LOCATION: UPPER WEST SIDE, NYC
OWNED/RENTED: OWNED
SIZE: 539 SQUARE FEET
TYPE: STUDIO IN A PREWAR, 6-STORY
APARTMENT BUILDING
YEARS LIVED IN: 3

*The signed photo of Loretta Young (opposite, bottom left) hangs in
the bathroom. The etching on the medicine cabinet mirror inspired the
wallpaper pattern. Curtis found a pattern from a 1940s Montgomery
Ward wallpaper sample book and replicated it with a stencil. He chose
colors that work well with the room's original black and peach tiles.
The sconce is from* Rejuvenation Lighting.

When we first saw Curtis's apartment, we weren't sure what to think. His furniture is pretty traditional, but his walls blew our minds. Never before had we seen such painstaking hand-painted mural and wall decoration outside the sets of a Broadway play or the work in a museum. Curtis's treatments make a phenomenal impact on the interior of his modest apartment. Discarding the notion that a wall has to be a solid color and is fit only for hanging a picture, Curtis has made his walls the pictures themselves. His mural of a street scene leads your eye right up to and into it. Walls are not the only surfaces that Curtis has decorated. He sees potential in places that others would not, such as the housing of his television and the imitation wallpaper in the kitchen and bathroom.

Lately, it hasn't been chic to inject this much ornamentation into a contemporary home, but this is so beautifully and lovingly done that it works. All of Curtis's wall treatments are masterpieces of creativity, talent, and diligence.

All of Curtis's wall treatments are masterpieces of creativity, talent, and diligence.

Painting the pattern on the kitchen walls required a handmade cardboard stencil, eight custom-ordered rubber stamps, and rolls and rolls of blue painter's tape. The design is perfectly executed and equally spaced on all the walls.

Curtis didn't hesitate to embellish this 1981 Zenith TV. He used Super Sculpey and an X-Acto to create the design. After curing it in the oven, he glued it to the TV and spray-painted the material red and gold to create a gold leaf look.

His furniture is pretty traditional, but his walls blew our minds.

curtis's
survey

Style

Late deco.

Inspiration

The inspiration came from my father's reaction to the Internet listing of the apartment when I was trying to decide among several options. The wrought iron railing and the step-down living room struck him as a very glamorous element and he could imagine Loretta Young sweeping down in a ball gown. So, as the choices narrowed, we called this apartment "Loretta." At the closing, my broker gave me a framed signed photograph of Loretta Young in a white bathrobe, which hangs in my peach-and-black art deco bathroom.

Favorite Element

The Murphy bed that I had installed, which is housed behind rolling bookcases in a wall unit that also contains a dresser and is clad in a warm, beautiful burled-maple-patterned laminate with a deco-friendly Biedermeier flavor.

Biggest Challenge

Prioritizing the various projects and deciding which ones to pour how much money into when.

What Friends Say

They say that it's elegant but comfortable.

Biggest Embarrassment

The bathtub is still in desperate need of reglazing, but whenever I do it, it will be in the same peach color, because I love the old art deco colors.

Proudest DIY

My living room mural that I based on a pair of 1950s paint-by-number paintings of Paris at night with wet streets. Martha Stewart thanked me on her show for "... sharing that wonderful idea!" I'm pretty proud of that.

Biggest Indulgence

The silk rug in the living room. ABC Carpet & Home's Bronx warehouse had it marked down more than half off its original $8,000 price, though at $3,000 it was still more than I was used to spending, but it feels wonderful under bare feet.

Best Advice

Listen to the architecture of the space, and make it work for you.

Dream Source

The Internet. Several of the best things came off eBay (dining room chairs, dining room chandelier, light diffusers for kitchen and entryway), but other things were the results of general Internet searches, and either tracking down local places that would order them or just ordering directly.

Using paint-by-number blue paint and a grid, Curtis replicated and seamlessly merged two paint-by-number Paris street scenes purchased on **eBay**. He then took the eBay paintings to **Janovic** and matched the twenty-four colors needed to re-create the original palette. After numbering every can of paint and every section of the mural with a paint number, he invited his friends over, one at a time, to help paint. The mural took four months to complete.

A second layer of baseboard molding, painted black, hides fluorescent lights that illuminate the mural. The lights rest on black egg-crate from **Edee.com**. The Oriental rug comes from **ABC** Carpet & Home's *Bronx warehouse. Curtis purchased the round leather chairs at the* **Door Store**, *and the oval art deco coffee table on* **eBay**.

The two middle panels of the wall unit (left)
slide open to access a Murphy bed from the
Murphy Bed Design Center.

"Listen to the
architecture
of the space…"

Curtis turned a wooden sculpture of a rope (left, top) by his uncle into a lamp. He topped it with a Bed Bath & Beyond shade.

To create the pattern on the dining room walls (left, middle), Curtis used a roller from Rollerwall overlapped with an off-the-rack stencil turned upside down. He taped off the stripes and painted the layered patterns in three shades of Benjamin Moore's Flowering Herb.

Curtis wanted the three-sided chair (left, bottom) to look like a lead Monopoly token, so he reupholstered it with pewter vinyl upholstery purchased at ABC Carpet & Home. He then painted the wood with a mixture of black oil-based paint and silver radiator paint.

RESOURCES

ABC CARPET & HOME: abchome.com

BED BATH & BEYOND: bedbathandbeyond.com

BENJAMIN MOORE: benjaminmoore.com

DOOR STORE: doorstore.com

EBAY: ebay.com

EDEE.COM: edee.com

GRAND METRO HARDWARE: 212.749.4281

JANOVIC: janovic.com

MURPHY BED DESIGN CENTER: 718.782.5197

REJUVENATION LIGHTING: rejuvenation.com

ROLLERWALL: rollerwall.com

photos by
evan
thomas

07.
dana's sunny logan square apartment

entrance

bedroom

closet

living room

dining room

kitchen

office

bathroom

storage

NAME: DANA JOY ALTMAN
PROFESSION: DESIGN/HOSPITALITY
CONSULTANT
LOCATION: LOGAN SQUARE, CHICAGO
OWNED/RENTED: RENTED
SIZE: 1,700 SQUARE FEET
TYPE: SINGLE-FAMILY HOME,
CIRCA 1902, CARVED INTO 3 UNITS
YEARS LIVED IN: 1

Dana's three-bedroom apartment stands out for the skill with which she has integrated the old and the new in a decidedly feminine way. Starting from scratch, she furnished her home in one year on a shoe-string budget, which is possible to do well in Chicago. She began with two pieces of furniture that she couldn't part with and purchased the rest from local sources, including the city's many antique malls. In every room, she mixed purchased furnishings with treasures from her youth and a supercool collection of contemporary art. Sunlight completes the effect. With windows on all three sides and a deck overlooking the garden, the apartment is always light and inviting. Dana inherited a good sense of style from her mother, whom she calls an "incredibly modern woman with amazing taste and vision." Items from her childhood include needlepoint pillows her mother made circa 1972. Dana had the pillows restuffed with down and the backs replaced. Many housewares are from the same era: Dansk wood bowls, enameled Copco oven-to-table cookware in great shapes and colors, and handmade earthenware bowls and serving pieces. An all-time favorite is her mother's brick red porcelain Villeroy & Boch china. "It was her wedding china," Dana says. "Okay, it was her third wedding . . . but it's still so hip."

...she has integrated the old and the new in a decidedly feminine way.

053

dana joy :: altman

The walnut and chrome credenza (left) from the Edgewater Antique Mall *holds a vintage lamp from the* Broadway Antique Market, *along with a growing collection of 1960s and '70s ceramics. The two silkscreen prints are by* Cody Hudson.

Dana discovered the 1960s sofa (right) at the Ark Thrift Shop. *She replaced the casters with metal cylinders to give the piece more of a 1970s feel. Her mother made the needle-point pillows. The radiator holds a vintage lamp and a work on paper by* Dan Devening.

survey

dana's

Style

Sunny, relaxed, plush, and colorful.

Inspiration

Creating a personal haven that reflects who I am right now. My other big inspiration is the natural world.

Favorite Element

The layout is wide and spacious, unlike a lot of older Chicago apartments. Also, my deck is pretty amazing; it overlooks the yard and is another room unto itself.

Biggest Challenge

Having the patience to let things come together slowly and thoughtfully.

What Friends Say

I hear all the time that the place just feels good or that it has good energy. I couldn't ask for a greater compliment.

Biggest Embarrassment

The entryway; a former tenant painted blood-red paint over wallpaper and I've yet to deal with it . . .

Proudest DIY

The gold-painted pressed-tin ceiling in the living room.

Biggest Indulgence

Buying the olive green leather couch for the bedroom was a huge luxury for me. My 1960s Nagel candelabra was also a mighty big splurge.

Best Advice

Take the time to find the things that really move you; don't just buy stuff to fill up space. Also, buy the best quality you can afford.

Dream Sources

Art galleries around the world, if only, and I'd love a shopping spree at Casati Gallery in Chicago or Todd Merrill in NYC any day of the week.

Luxurious, eclectic, personal—Dana's living room has all these qualities.
She painted the walls Ralph Lauren Studio White *and used Chromatone*
Latex Metallic Gold on the original pressed tin ceiling. She bought the
iconic Eames *rocker at the* Design Within Reach *warehouse sale. The red*
chair is from Knoll, *and the painting above it is by* Dan Devening. *Dana*
picked up the two-tiered coffee table at the Ark Thrift Shop.

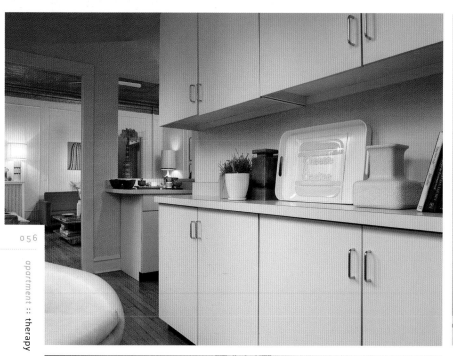

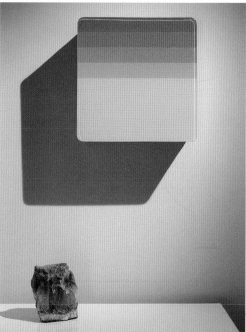

A wall sculpture (above) by Josue Pellot hangs over a chunk of emerald calcite from Dave's Down to Earth Rock Shop.

(opposite, top) Dana and her boyfriend rescued the turquoise metal D from a building demolition. It adds a lighthearted touch to the bedroom. She chose cool colors, such as Ralph Lauren Alium Green for the walls and the green Cecchi e Cecchi throw from Bedside Manor. The natural light and warm wood keep the palette from feeling cold. The bedroom is spacious enough to accommodate the green leather sofa Dana picked up at a Design Within Reach warehouse sale. A Zebra pillow from CB2 is displayed on a vintage Heywood Wakefield dresser, one of only two pieces that she brought from her previous home. The other is her dining table.

Dana's kitchen (above, top) is sunny thanks to the bright walls and south-facing windows, which overlook her room-sized deck. Vintage housewares include the funky cheese-and-cracker plate from Epicene and a yellow Haeger vase from the Ravenswood Antique Mart.

A ruby red Knoll chair (above) anchors a corner of the dining room. Dana found the rounded Parsons-style table at Mt. Sinai Resale Shop. The chairs, which suit it well, are finds from another resale shop, the Brown Elephant. The Flos standing lamp is from the Design Within Reach warehouse sale.

(opposite, bottom) One of Dana's prized possessions is the 1960s modular Nagel candelabra from Modern Times, which can be rearranged into different configurations. She found the rya rug at the Ravenswood Antique Market. The large-format photograph is part of Ryan Robinson's Snowbirds series.

RESOURCES

ARK THRIFT SHOP: arkchicago.org

BEDSIDE MANOR: bedsidemanorltd.com

BROADWAY ANTIQUE MARKET: bamchicago.com

BROWN ELEPHANT: howardbrown.org

CB2: cb2.com

DAN DEVENING: deveningprojects.com

DAVE'S DOWN TO EARTH ROCK SHOP:

davesdowntoearthrockshop.com

DESIGN WITHIN REACH: dwr.com

EDGEWATER ANTIQUE MALL:

edgewaterantiquemall.com

EPICENE: 773.395.8171

JOSUE PELLOT: josuepellot.com

KNOLL: knoll.com

MODERN TIMES: moderntimeschicago.com

MT. SINAI RESALE SHOP: 773.935.1434

RALPH LAUREN PAINT: rlhome.polo.com

RAVENSWOOD ANTIQUE MART: 773.271.3700

RYAN ROBINSON: ryanrobinson.com

08.

entrance

dante's industriousness

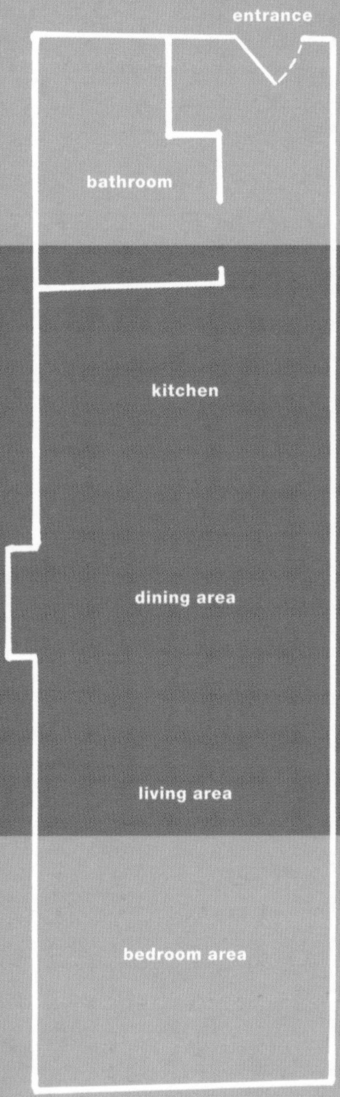

bathroom

kitchen

NAME: DANTE PAUWELS

PROFESSION: HANDBAG DESIGNER

LOCATION: CHINATOWN/SOHO, NYC

OWNED/RENTED: RENTED

dining area

SIZE: 525 SQUARE FEET

TYPE: LOFT IN AN EARLY 20TH-CENTURY

INDUSTRIAL BUILDING

MONTHS LIVED IN: 6

living area

bedroom area

Trixie, Dante's dog, greets you at the front door. The old floors were refinished and stained dark brown to unify and warm up the space.

Dante made the light table from polypropylene plastic sheets held together with snaps. A light and switch are inside. The lamp came from a thrift store. The shade, from Just Shades, *cost many times the price of the lamp.*

We have the pleasure of sharing offices with Dante. So when she decided to lease more office space in our building with the aim of turning it into her home, we had front-row seats on the transformation. The grim space, divided into small rooms lit by fluorescent fixtures, had been occupied by a skin-care spa. Dante saw potential where others might not, but no one could deny it was in a great location – fifty steps from our offices and on the edge of SoHo.

Demolishing the spa took two days. Then the landlord installed a new bathroom, new lighting, and Dante's careful selection of IKEA products, all of which make this a fully functioning home. When they painted the walls a warm off-white and Dante moved in her belongings, her beautiful home finally took shape.

Dante has a knack for knowing how to play up a room's strengths. She arranged everything to highlight the tall ceilings and windows. The curtains, track lights, spacious walls, and stained floor create a sense of roominess and elegance. Although Dante went to IKEA for the practical things, her own collection of lively furniture gives her home character.

Working with a long, open space is tough, but she has carefully divided it to create inviting circulation and to hide the least sightly elements. She packed a great deal of storage against a front wall behind curtains, tucked the kitchen into a corner, and used chairs and bookcases to guide traffic through the room and toward the windows.

This shows that you can build a home anywhere. Now Dante comes to work with her coffee mug and goes home each day for lunch, while we still commute.

Biggest Embarrassment

The heat for this apartment comes out of a big, ugly blower by the entry door. I tried to cover it over with a billowy mesh curtain, but it looked like a ghost. I just have to live with it.

Proudest DIY

I made all of the curtains in the space out of leftover bag fabrics. I think they work nicely, and certainly cover loads of otherwise unsightly storage spaces.

Biggest Indulgence

The big fluffy rug in the center of the living room. I'm just waiting for the dog to foul it in some way.

Best Advice

Don't spend a lot of money on anything you won't use for the rest of your life.

Dream Sources

Jonathan Adler, Chelsea Passage at Barneys, ABC Carpet & Home, and Moss.

dante's

survey

Style

Vintage modern meets French vintage meets books meets color!

Inspiration

The inspiration was to create a home that would morph easily into a work space. I plan to move out of this space within the year and make it the work space for my business, Dante Beatrix. Everything that I bought was with this in mind.

Favorite Element

I like all of the warm red and orange patterns and the way they work together.

Biggest Challenge

Figuring out a way to create separate areas without walls. The low row of bookcases is key: these separate the bedroom area from the living area without cutting out the light source from the windows.

What Friends Say

They say that it's warm and inviting, and that it looks like me.

To remedy the lack of closets, Dante created a twenty-foot wall of storage and work space and made curtains to cover it all up. She painted the walls with Benjamin Moore's Elephant Tusk and the trim and ceiling with Decorator's White. Behind the curtains are two full bays of clothing, a sewing corner, sewing supplies, and bolts of fabric. The dining table is from a thrift store in Menlo Park, California.

The cabinets and shelves (opposite) are from IKEA. The top two shelves hold Dansk enamel pieces that Dante accumulated from various antique stores and patterned enamelware from a store in Amsterdam. "I brought back everything I could carry," she says. To the right of the shelves hangs a watercolor, Butter Butter Butter, by Apartment Therapy's Maxwell Gillingham-Ryan.

Dante combined silver objects and turquoise dishware on one shelf (below, left).

The stack of pillows (below, right) sits in front of low bookshelves that separate Dante's bedroom from the living area. She found some while on vacation in Turkey, others at a fabric store in the Garment District that sells imported textiles.

This shows that you can build a home anywhere

Dante bought the pink lawn furniture at an antique store in Menlo Park just after she finished graduate school. She repainted the metal and re-covered the cushions with upholstery-weight velveteen. The red couch is a find from the Hell's Kitchen Flea Market. *Dante reupholstered it with a vintage wool fabric she used to make clutches. The coffee table is from the* Brimfield Antique Market, *and the luxurious shag carpet from* Crate & Barrel. *The* IKEA *bookshelves are just high enough to conceal Dante's bed next to the windows. The shelves came with legs, but Dante removed them so the unit looks like a solid wall, rather than a piece of furniture.*

Dante's curtains couldn't have been easier
to make: she hemmed three sides and sewed
a channel for the curtain rod. She found
the chair abandoned outside an antique
market and repainted it glossy white.

In the absence of a wall, the bookshelves
(below) create a private space for the
bedroom. The white sheets with a red scallop
design are from Garnet Hill, and the duvet
cover and matching pillowcases are from
IKEA. The bedside lamp is from Dante's
Great-Aunt Nernie. Dante found a new shade
for it at Just Shades.

photos by
evan
thomas

09.

david's andersonville apartment

NAME: DAVID HOPKINS

PROFESSION: DESIGNER

LOCATION: ANDERSONVILLE, CHICAGO

OWNED/RENTED: RENTED

SIZE: 1,200 SQUARE FEET

TYPE: 2-BEDROOM IN A CIRCA-1910 BUILDING WITH 4 FLATS

YEARS LIVED IN: 2

David's foyer (opposite) brings together objects high and low. A red-flocked Jesus coin bank, a housewarming present, stands in front of a print by Marc Chagall framed by Armand Lee Framing. The sideboard from his mother's basement also holds a Crate & Barrel vase filled with painted branches from Jayson Home and Garden. The walls are painted with Livingston Gold by Benjamin Moore.

David calls his style "high pomp."

We chose David's home not only because it is a beautiful interpretation of a traditional Chicago apartment, but also because it was a hit with our readers. Why such enthusiasm? We think David's apartment is among several in this book that signal a shift over the past eight years or so from more spartan, loftlike interiors without trim or color to richer and warmer interiors with deep colors and traditional designs.

To architecture that is traditional, David has brought a style that is a riff on the traditional. Each room fluidly mixes old pieces and vintage-style fixtures with new furniture. The richly colored walls make a surprisingly effective backdrop for his collection of contemporary art. The effect is fresh and stimulating. David calls his style "high pomp," and we like that as a tagline for similar styles we've seen in other apartments.

As you tour David's apartment, you may find yourself slowing down to look at the many varied and interesting objects. This reflects the careful process he followed to choose everything, particularly the artwork.

David rescued the 1950s chair (above) from an alley and re-covered it in fabric by Donghia. *The Parallel Lines desk is from* Quinlans. *The lamp, from the* Brown Elephant, *has a custom-painted shade. The painting is a "reclaimed" piece of art by* Babe Nasset.

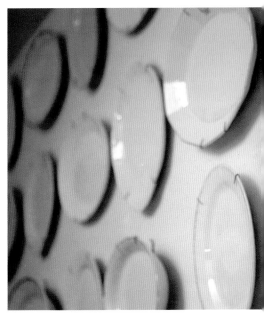

The vintage platters come from many sources. The ones David calls "really cool" are from Scout.

*(opposite, top) The red armchair is a 1930s Cook County office chair that David purchased from **Scout**. He found the gold armchair in his mother's basement and re-covered it with paisley velvet by **Kravet**. He snatched up the coffee table at an estate sale in Glencoe.*

*(opposite, bottom) Having oiled the **IKEA** wooden counter units weekly, David says they are now water- and stain-proof. The wall-mounted metal dish rack and knife holder are also from **IKEA**. David found the big bowl on the counter at the **Brown Elephant** thrift shop.*

david's
survey

Style

An eclectic mix of furnishings that don't drain my wallet but reflect my "high pomp" personality.

Inspiration

Can be summed up as wanting lots of crap on the walls.

Favorite Element

The moderately creepy baby head sculpture on the fireplace mantel. I fell in love with it at the artist's studio and told him to hold it for me. Unbeknownst to me, my good friend went in and bought it as a gift; I was very bummed out when the artist would not sell it to me but was overjoyed when I opened up a package a few months later.

Biggest Challenge

Working in all of the trim details in the space. I love the arts and crafts detailing, but it made the rooms feel very busy when the walls were all white.

What Friends Say

It usually revolves around it being a little too perfect. I get a lot of "Martha Stewart" comments, but I think I have my own style.

Biggest Embarrassment

The ever-present pile of dry cleaning heaped in a corner of the dressing room.

Proudest DIY

It's a toss-up. I built a platform in the sunroom to level out a very uneven floor to make the space usable. I also love the huge lampshade that I hung over a very unattractive foyer ceiling fixture.

Biggest Indulgence

My decision to turn the master bedroom (twice as big as the second bedroom) into a walk-in closet and dressing room. I would not let it be photographed because it always looks like a nightmare, but it helps me keep the rest of the place tidy.

Best Advice

Take time to curate the objects you have and look to lots of different sources. Regardless if you go to Holly Hunt or to IKEA, if you buy every object in a space from one resource, your home will absolutely lack character.

Dream Sources

A mixture of objects from Holly Hunt, Pavilion Antiques on Damen Avenue in Chicago, and Swallowtail in San Francisco. Holly Hunt does a wide range of well-crafted items, Pavilion shows pedigreed pieces from the '20s to the '70s imported from Europe, and Swallowtail mixes some of the most unusual stuff (think original phrenology heads and taxidermy goats) I have ever seen for sale.

The baby head sculpture (opposite, top) is by Jay Strommen, *who exhibits at* Perimeter Gallery *and has been featured at* SOFA Expo. *The 1950s architect's lamp is from* Scout, *and the glass bottles are by* Venini. *David bought the print by* Jae Non *at the* School of the Art Institute of Chicago *annual sale.*

David had the custom headboard (opposite, bottom) made from a 1940s Italian tapestry purchased on eBay. The bedding by Isaac Mizrahi *is from* Target. *He found the nightstand at* Brown Elephant *and the lamp at* Crate & Barrel. *David chose* Benjamin Moore Pampas Grass *for the walls.*

RESOURCES

David's mother's basement was the source for several pieces, including the dining room chairs (below, left), which Eli Wyn Upholstery *re-covered. Twin sconces from* Crate & Barrel *frame the doorway. David repurposed the curtains from a previous residence and found the blinds and tablecloth at* Target.

Over the bathroom mirror (below, right) from Target, *David installed a light fixture from* Restoration Hardware. *The striped shower curtain was custom-made to fit the extra-tall space. He found the soap dispenser in the discount bin at* Bed Bath & Beyond. *The print in the hallway reflected in the mirror is* Moonlight Serenade *by* Jacob Walker.

ARMAND LEE FRAMING: armandlee.com
BED BATH & BEYOND: bedbathandbeyond.com
BENJAMIN MOORE: benjaminmoore.com
BROWN ELEPHANT: howardbrown.org
CRATE & BARREL: crateandbarrel.com
DONGHIA: donghia.com
EBAY: eBay.com
ELI WYN UPHOLSTERY: 773.276.4441
HOLLY HUNT: hollyhunt.com
IKEA: ikea.com
JAYSON HOME AND GARDEN: jaysonhome-garden.com
KRAVET: kravet.com
PAVILION ANTIQUES: pavilionantiques.com
PERIMETER GALLERY: perimetergallery.com
QUINLANS: 773-394-3433
RESTORATION HARDWARE: restorationhardware.com
SCHOOL OF THE ART INSTITUTE OF CHICAGO: saic.edu
SCOUT: scoutchicago.com
SOFAEXPO: sofaexpo.com
SWALLOWTAIL: swallowtailsf.com
TARGET: target.com
VENINI: venini.it

photos by
david schafer

10.

david and im's
onespace

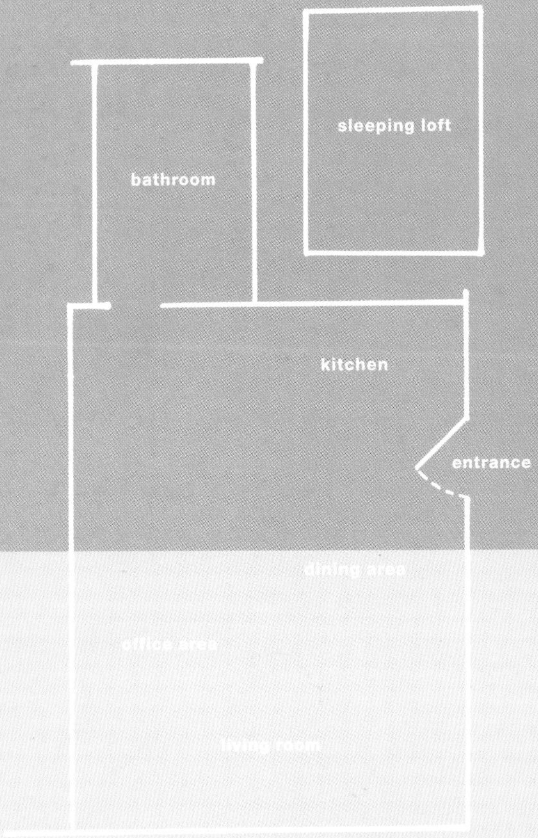

sleeping loft

bathroom

kitchen

entrance

dining area

office area

living room

NAME: DAVID AND IM
PROFESSION: ARCHITECTS
LOCATION: DOWNTOWN SAN DIEGO
OWNED/RENTED: RENTED
SIZE: 426 SQUARE FEET
TYPE: LOFT IN A NEW 4-STORY
BUILDING WITH 9 UNITS
YEARS LIVED IN: 3

David and Im chose a very small apartment in San Diego — a city where finding a spacious rental is usually not a problem — because the place is extremely affordable and offers them tons of light. Before they decided to move in with each other, they had lived in roomier homes. OneSpace, the name they chose for their remarkable shared home, packs the contents of David's former 800-square-foot residence and Im's 500-square-foot residence into a 426-square-foot downtown loft.

The previous tenant, a consummate urban bachelor, was satisfied living in a minimalist setting, but David and Im had more intensive requirements and much more ambitious design goals. They had to create a good deal of storage, and they wanted OneSpace to seem as if it contained separate rooms. Given the high ceilings, they knew that the solution was to design up.

Paying less for rent than when they lived separately, David and Im had a little extra money each month. They carefully considered the value of each improvement and alternated between splurging in some areas and going cheap in others.

According to Im, "the smallest detail can sculpt the overall shape of a space." When you tour OneSpace, you'll see numerous fine details interspersed with straight-ahead practical solutions that give the loft the feeling of a two-story home. Everything seems to have its perfect place, but David and Im say that they are "continually fine-tuning their methods of living."

"THE SMALLEST DETAIL
CAN SCULPT THE
OVERALL SHAPE
OF A SPACE"

(previous page) A white curtain — made in Bangkok, Im's home city, while she and David vacationed there — hides all of their belongings. They bought a lot of white cotton fabric to avoid gaps between the two panels and hung the curtains from two overlapping hospital tracks. The tracks, called Click Ease, are from InPro.

David and Im sourced materials for the storage wall from Home Depot, Industrial Metal Supply, *and specialty lumberyards such as* Dixie Line *and* Frost Hardwood *that stock unusual sizes such as six-by-ten-foot sheets of MDF up to one inch thick. From local sailboat shops, they bought components designed for cramped quarters. David and Im went to* McMaster-Carr *for the stainless steel shelf fasteners. Because the nuts and bolts are exposed, they wanted hardware that is both attractive and resilient. The various storage boxes are from the* Container Store.

Proudest DIY

It was all DIY—most often with four hands, but sometimes six.

Biggest Indulgence

Our books.

Best Advice

Don't let gravity stop you.

Dream Source

Droog Design.

david and im's
survey

Style

Hyperfunction.

Inspiration

Charles and Ray Eames, tools, and necessity.

Favorite element

Our kitchen and our Design Within Reach Eames Aluminum Group Lounge Chair and Ottoman.

Biggest Challenge

Combining David's 800-square-foot loft with Im's 500-square-foot apartment into 426 square feet of space.

What Friends Say

"Is the rest of your apartment behind that white curtain?"

Biggest Embarrassment

"No, actually it's just a big closet behind that white curtain."

David and Im made such efficient use of vertical space that the upper wall of the kitchen area serves as storage for extra seating. For lighting, they went to Lowe's and chose MR-11 Track Lighting, then hot-wired noncompatible fixtures above the sink to work with this system. Throughout the space, they installed various transformers from Light Bulbs Unlimited. The pair of IKEA task lights on the dining table was initially meant to be temporary.

David and Im's impeccable organization is in full view in the kitchen (opposite). They made the shelves from lengths of MDF held by aluminum L brackets. The four-by-ten-foot stainless steel sheets for the counter, as well as for the storage wall, came from Industrial Metal Supply. A friend at Vincent Designs in San Diego offered them work space to weld the brackets and cut the sheets to size.

given the high ceilings, they knew that the solution was to design up.

The only pieces that David and Im did not fabricate are the **La-Z-Boy** *Snap couch by* **Todd Oldham** *and the early 1970s Eames chairs (above), which they received as gifts. They disassembled an existing planter on the balcony, made it narrower, and added a stainless steel top. The interior provides storage for camping gear and raw materials. The top makes an ideal bar when entertaining outdoors. For large parties, they move the dining table onto the balcony. Looking into OneSpace from the large balcony provides a different view of the main living area (bottom). Like the kitchen shelves, the dining table is made from MDF and brackets. David and Im built the coffee table in architecture school in 1999.*

They stacked cardboard scraps on edge, trimmed them, and then had them assembled and laminated. The sisal rug is from the **Crate & Barrel Outlet.** *The flooring throughout the loft is concrete slab.*

The ladder to the sleeping loft was the most planned-out part of the project. Alternating treads are six-by-ten-inch plates of three-sixteenth-inch steel welded to one-and-one-half-inch steel angles. The angles are through-bolted to the two-by-twelve-foot stringer, which in turn is attached to the storage wall.

The sleeping loft has a ceiling height of only four feet, so David and Im kept the space as simple as possible. They carpeted the loft with green House Pet Flor modular carpet tiles. The apartment is painted throughout in Home Depot's Behr Bright White.

RESOURCES

CONTAINER STORE: containerstore.com
CRATE & BARREL: crateandbarrel.com
DIXIE LINE: dixieline.com
DROOG DESIGN: droogdesign.nl
FLOR: florcatalog.com
FROST HARDWOOD: frosthardwood.com
HOME DEPOT: homedepot.com
IKEA: ikea.com
INDUSTRIAL METAL SUPPLY: capitolmetals.com
INPRO: inprocorp.com
LA-Z-BOY: lazboy.com
LIGHT BULBS UNLIMITED: lightbulbsunlimited.net
LOWE'S: lowes.com
MCMASTER-CARR: mcmaster.com
VINCENT DESIGNS: vincentdesigns.com

photos by
jill
slater

11.

dixie's vintage carnival

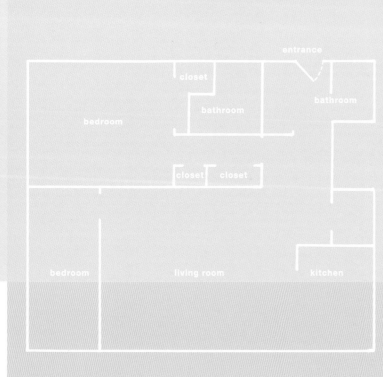

NAME: DIXIE FELDMAN
PROFESSION: EDITORIAL DIRECTOR
LOCATION: MIDTOWN
MANHATTAN, NYC
OWNED/RENTED: OWNED
SIZE: 1,100 SQUARE FEET
TYPE: 1-BEDROOM IN PREWAR
12-STORY CO-OP
YEARS LIVED IN: LESS THAN A YEAR

she prefers to listen to
her inner yearnings rather
than follow any style piped in
by the mainstream shelter
magazines and catalogs.

Dixie represents the epitome of a funky and totally personal approach to interior design. As she herself admits, "my decor could be called stuff other people no longer want." Far from being behind the times or lazy, she is a rigorous romantic with a passion for very specific genres. She also loves to juxtapose objects of different styles and textures. Although some may see the cumulative effect as carnival-like or overwhelming, Dixie finds it perfectly comfortable.

"While my decor speaks to my romanticism," Dixie says, "my apartment is also immensely pragmatic." She removed a wall that originally separated the living room from a bedroom and created a large living area where she cooks, eats, and works alongside her five parrots and dog. The remaining, smaller room is her master bedroom, where a trundle bed suffices for now until she replaces it. Some people would have balked at removing a bedroom and thereby lowering the value of the apartment, but Dixie vastly improved the space by making a long, sunny main room best suited to her uses. Dixie says that she prefers to listen to her inner yearnings rather than follow any style piped in by the mainstream shelter magazines and catalogs, and she encourages others to do the same.

Dixie's dining room table is from the Hell's Kitchen Flea Market, *and the Philippe Starck chairs are from* Design Within Reach.

(left) *The floating bookshelves are from* Design Within Reach. *The bold chandelier from* Greatchandeliers.com *delineates the dining area of the large living room space.*

(opposite) *The chests, tables, table/magazine rack, and 1930s* Heywood Wakefield *nightstand all hail from the* Hell's Kitchen Flea Market. *Dixie found the red bookcases on the sidewalk. The* Eames *chair and ottoman and the faux leopard armchair are gifts from Dixie's mom.* Philippe Starck *designed the gnomes and ghost chairs for the St. Martin's Hotel, where Dixie first saw them.*

dixie's
survey

Style

I call it "Girlie Kitsch Moderne." It is a mix of over-the-top femininity, sylvan woodland creatures, Hollywood glam, and midcentury modern classics.

Inspiration

I feel fearless about surrounding myself with objects and art that speak to me. I'm drawn to things that connote innocence, glamour, naïveté, and sexuality.

Favorite Element

My fantastic large Moses Soyer painting of a beautiful redhead in my foyer (one of several Soyers), coupled with my five parrots and my dog, Lulu. Oh, and my taxidermy duckling, Abraham.

Biggest Challenge

I drained my bank account buying my apartment. From here on it's a work in progress. The kitchen and bathrooms remain largely the way they were when I moved in. Also, the living room is so large I'm not sure how to arrange the furniture to fit the space.

What Friends Say

The consensus is that it looks like my brain threw up.

Biggest Embarrassment

The two bathrooms are done in a style I would NOT have chosen (though to make lemonade out of lemons I turned the "guest bathroom" into a "Boy's Bathroom" with lots of breast mugs, *Playboy* stuff, pinups, etc.).

Proudest DIY

The whole apartment really: the wall colors, the paintings, the decor. For example, I took some flea market snapshots of a 1950s woman serially stripping next to (inexplicably) a bicycle and framed them, and turned an old Eddie Cantor board game into a cute table with pom-poms.

Biggest Indulgence

Some might say six chandeliers in an apartment are "too much," but I'm hankering to get MORE.

Best Advice

Be yourself. It's always good advice, in every arena. Also, I've gotten MUCH better at editing. My last apartment was, as the French say, *de trop*, but now, even though I have twice the space, I have half the stuff—and much more blank wall space!

Dream Source

I love midcentury modern classics and have started slowly, with an Eames chair and ottoman here, a fine art piece there.

Dixie bought trophies at flea markets and had them professionally inscribed with her name. Another trophy in the apartment reads "Dixie Feldman, Never Shot Anyone."

She picked up the trundle bed at a showroom sample sale at **Sleepy's** and is using it until she figures out what bed she really wants here. Her collections, accumulated over years of exploring flea markets, include 1950s figural lamps, Childcraft puppets, a taxidermied duckling, woodland creatures, and several rugs that depict cowboys, bowling, and Snow White. Dixie turns to **eBay** for great 1930s movie memorabilia. The walls are painted **Benjamin Moore's** Honolulu Blue.

Dixie's grandmother painted the nude, which hangs next to a 1930s pulp fiction poster. Dixie refers to her paint-by-numbers collection as "mechanized folk art." She found the paintings at flea markets and on eBay.

(opposite) Dixie bought the mannequin heads at the Pier Antiques Show in New York, held every November and March. Collections from the 1930s through 1950s continue from the living area into Dixie's bedroom. Some of the objects are displayed on two Heywood Wakefield chests. She found the antlers at the Hell's Kitchen Flea Market and uses them for hanging jewelry. The Carnival Chalkware, arranged in a row just below the ceiling, were originally given as carnival prizes in the 1920s through 1940s. They are made of chalk and are extremely fragile. Each began life with a story: "Some sailor or girl he won it for cherished it," Dixie says. "It touches me."

Dixie and her parrot Butch.

RESOURCES

BENJAMIN MOORE: benjaminmoore.com

DESIGN WITHIN REACH: dwr.com

EBAY: ebay.com

GREATCHANDELIERS.COM: greatchandeliers.com

HELL'S KITCHEN FLEA MARKET: hellskitchenfleamarket.com

HEYWOOD WAKEFIELD: heywood-wakefield.com

PIER ANTIQUES SHOW: stellashows.com

SLEEPY'S: sleepys.com

photos by
goldberg /esto

12.

gideon and tracy's pocket knife

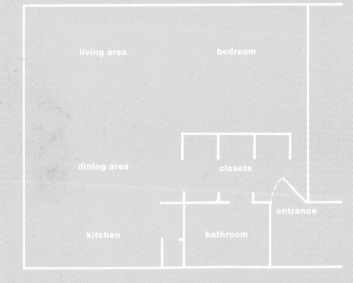

living area

bedroom

dining area

closets

entrance

kitchen

bathroom

NAME: GIDEON AND TRACY

PROFESSION: SHIPPING INDUSTRY EXECUTIVE (GIDEON) AND INTERIOR DESIGNER (TRACY)

LOCATION: JERSEY CITY, NEW JERSEY

OWNED/RENTED: OWNED

SIZE: 530 SQUARE FEET

TYPE: STUDIO IN LATE-19TH-CENTURY OFFICE BUILDING

YEARS LIVED IN: 5

The Pocket Knife blew us away. Based on the idea of a pocket knife, whose blades open and retract and serve many functions, Gideon and Tracy's home tucks everything into one room. This is a rare feat, but the apartment still manages to provide privacy, openness, and stunning interior views.

The Pocket Knife photographs well because it's laid out well and the floor plan maximizes the sight lines. Gideon and Tracy built all the storage and seating along the edges so the apartment is not cluttered with unnecessary walls. Gideon constructed a sophisticated rotating divider, the "pocket knife," which defines and transforms each living space — kitchen, dining area, living area, and bedroom.

We love the black floors. Something about black floors warms up and grounds a space. Gideon points out that using a dark stain makes even the cheapest oak floors look "sexy," and that the dark color causes the floor to "drop away" and gives the space an illusion of height.

On first glance, you might think that it's easy to make your home this nice if you have a lot to spend, but this wasn't a high-end project. Gideon and Tracy did most of the work themselves over a long period, and nothing is prohibitively fancy. Sure, they spent some money (a good investment!), but the genius is all in the planning.

On first glance, you might think it's easy to make your home this nice if you have a lot to spend, but this wasn't a high-end project.

The hanging light is Venini *Murano glass. Gideon and Tracy purchased it at* Upstairs Downtown Antiques.

gideon and tracy's
survey

Style

Warm modern.

Inspiration

The tools from a pocket knife.

Favorite Element

The movable wall.

Biggest Challenge

The old building itself with its poor
condition. The windows, ceiling
beams, and floor joists were rotted
and burned in places.

What Friends Say

"What color green is that?"

Biggest Embarrassment

We could not get the wall through the
front door, so we had to winch it up
from the roof and through the windows
in two pieces.

Proudest DIY

The dining table.

Biggest Indulgence

The upholstery on the window
banquettes.

Best Advice

Benjamin Moore HC81 (Manchester
Tan); it's the magic color.

Dream Sources

Modhaus.com and Benjamin Moore.

...based on the idea of a pocket knife, whose blades open and retract...

The pocket knife has been rotated to reveal the kitchen. Gideon and Tracy recessed the upper cabinets, from **IKEA**, into the wall and trimmed them along the bottom with an aluminum strip. Gideon installed lighting that illuminates the glass shelves and doors from within. The lower cabinets are custom-made. Gideon painted the wood cabinets and the wood counter with white **Benjamin Moore Satin Impervo** (oil-based paint). He used marine-grade wood and glue for the counter so it would withstand water if repainted periodically. The kitchen wall is **Benjamin Moore's Palladian Blue**, a medium green. Gideon likes to use subtle colors that seem to change in different light.

Gideon designed the solid cherry din-ing table. The Planner group chairs are by Paul McCobb. Gideon likes them because they are among the few classic modern chairs that haven't been ubiq-uitously knocked off. He bought one at Upstairs Downtown and the other at Planet Oranj. Both were in poor condi-tion and were refinished professionally in Benjamin Moore's Greenmount Silk. The living room features a Bau-haus chair designed by Franz Singer, one of Gideon's treasured possessions. He bought it from an antiques dealer and had the springs retied and the upholstery repaired.

The pocket knife can be rotated to enlarge the bedroom area. Gideon chose the simplest platform bed avail-able at West Elm because he wanted it to disappear into the floor and the wall behind it. He bolted the bed to the wall, which is cherry veneer plywood screwed onto a plywood backing. The cherry band that runs at about the height of a headboard across the bedroom wall hides the seam in the plywood sheets. Gideon let the stainless steel screws show in vertical stripes every four feet — an intentional, low-cost solution that looks handsome. The standing lamp is from IKEA. The shell chair is from Modernica.

(below, left) The section of the pocket knife above the TV is made of corrugated polycarbonate from Canal Plastics. Tracy and Gideon chose linen roman shades for all of the windows. Gideon built seating to hide the heating baseboards. He had the cushions cut to size and covered in canvas. The grates below the cushioned seating allow heat into the apartment. The built-ins, including the bookshelves along the far wall, and the ceiling are painted Benjamin Moore's Manchester Tan. Gideon calls it the magic color. Depending on the light, it appears dark gray to almost white. "It's a light phenomenon more than a paint color," he says.

(below, right) Gideon used plywood and MDF for the base of the pocket knife. It rotates on a large gate hinge from Lowe's. The leg that rotates has a big rubber caster. Gideon painted the entire unit Benjamin Moore's Greenmount Silk. He refinished the floor with the cheapest common oak he could find at Home Depot, stained it with black walnut Minwax, and then covered it with several layers of polyurethane to "make it look sexy."

Gideon and Tracy had two IKEA *shag rugs sewn together by their dry cleaner. Gideon painted the brick wall his favorite color, Benjamin Moore's White Dove — a white that has a lot of brown and yellow. Gideon's grandfather wore the framed baseball shirt when he played for City College in the 1930s.*

The X-base coffee table for Widdicomb by T. H. Robsjohn-Gibbings is from Modhaus. Gideon added a grommet hole in the cabinetry to hide the wiring of the IKEA lamp.

The beams are the tops of the closets, which separate the bedroom from the front door. The closets create a hallway that prevents you from seeing the entire apartment upon entering. For the beams, Gideon searched for just the right chocolate brown. He chose Ralph Lauren *over his favorite brand, Benjamin Moore.*

The fireplace, though usable, is mainly aesthetic. Gideon had a wrought iron grill custom-made for his new fireplace design.

RESOURCES

BENJAMIN MOORE: benjaminmoore.com

CANAL PLASTICS: canalplasticscenter.com

HOME DEPOT: homedepot.com

IKEA: ikea.com

LOWE'S: lowes.com

MODERNICA: modernica.net

MODHAUS: modhaus.com

PLANET ORANJ: planetoranj.com

RALPH LAUREN PAINT: rlhome.polo.com

UPSTAIRS DOWNTOWN ANTIQUES: 212.989.8715

WEST ELM: westelm.com

photos by
gregory
han

13.

gregory and emily's silverlake sanctuary

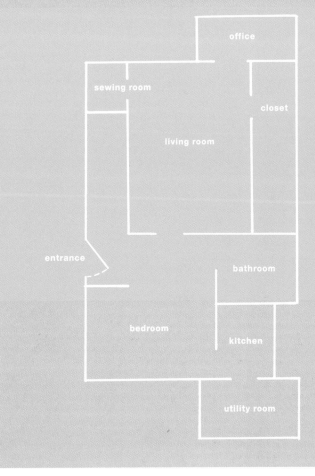

office

sewing room

closet

living room

entrance

bathroom

bedroom

kitchen

utility room

NAME: GREGORY HAN AND EMILY HO
PROFESSION: SENIOR GRAPHIC DESIGNER
AT A TOY COMPANY (GREGORY) AND
LIBRARIAN AT GETTY INSTITUTE (EMILY)
LOCATION: SILVERLAKE, LOS ANGELES
OWNED/RENTED: RENTED
SIZE: 639 SQUARE FEET
TYPE: 1-BEDROOM IN A FOURPLEX
BUILT IN 1917
YEARS LIVED IN: 2.5

After seeing this amazing apartment in our *smallest coolest apartment contest 2006*, we hired Gregory — sight unseen — to be one of the editors of *AT:LA* a few months later. Gregory and Emily have taken a traditional craftsman-style interior and made it bright and contemporary, without removing any of the traditional details. Their use of color throughout makes a huge impact. They selected a bright white for the molding. Others might have gone for off-white or a softer white, but this white is close to photographer's white and very reflective, creating an especially modern look with a slight edge. Going against the tendency most people have to use warm colors for the majority of their home, Gregory and Emily picked blue and green and a hot yellow. The strong contrast between the blue and yellow in particular gives their rooms a pop feeling and undercuts any suggestion that the decor might be traditional. Where did these colors come from? We think Gregory and Emily were inspired by their large robot anime collection, which seems right at home against the walls.

Most people struggle to house their collections in an orderly, handsome way. We believe that if you want a collection, you have to honor it and give it a featured place in your home. Gregory and Emily are perfect examples of how to edit a great collection. "The studio," says Emily, "has really taught us to live better with less . . . an especially notable accomplishment considering our bibliomania and propensity for collecting." As they have pared down their belongings, they've let their collections grow and have used them to decorate their home tastefully. In the end, we can all learn from their home and profit from their philosophy: "Buy less, buy better, and buy only what you love."

One of the apartment's many original built-in wood and glass cabinets displays this small found-object sculpture (far left) by Souther Salazar.

Emily transformed one of the smaller rooms into her sewing room (left). She found the Bertoia chair in a San Francisco Dumpster, and inherited a blue sewing machine from her Grandma. The room is full of supplies, tidily stored thanks to shelves from Home Depot *and containers from* IKEA *and* Zipper.

Gregory now works with toys professionally, but he has always been a collector of designer vinyls (left) — little figures aimed at adult collectors — sold in Hong Kong, Japan, and the United States.

*(opposite, top) Against the white, which repeats in every room, Gregory and Emily use strong colors. The white unites the home, and each color creates a distinct living area. Gregory bought the 1971 **Bang & Olufsen** stereo system on **eBay** from a former Playboy executive. The corner is occupied by **Tom Dixon**'s Jack lamp. The piece hanging above the TV is a stretched canvas covered with **Crate & Barrel** fabric, a DIY project.*

gregory and emily's
survey

Style

An assemblage of curiosities, color, and delicious candy. Toybox modern. Eames meets Miyazaki. We're all over the place but strive for freshness over clutter.

Inspiration

Our collections of toys, books, and artwork helped create the visual palette we used to paint and develop the interior. We took color cues from our favorite toys, vintage and retro fabrics, old Avon bath and body containers, and various illustrations, prints, and books/graphic novels. We think we have successfully balanced modern and vintage aesthetics, creating something that is playful and fresh.

Favorite Element

The color in each room (all nine of them). Each has a distinct feel thanks to the interaction of the interior colors with the lighting, whether from sunlight during the day or from the interior lighting in the evening.

Biggest Challenge

All of the little rooms and closets were challenging because we had to get rid of some of our furniture and many of our belongings to keep the rooms uncluttered—which was actually quite liberating.

What Friends Say

They can't believe it is the same space, transformed from peeling paint and dingy floors to something clean and bright. People also ask us to help them with their apartments!

Biggest Embarrassment

The kitchen and bathroom floors, which are covered in ugly vinyl "tile" sheets that look perpetually dirty. They just don't fit in with the rest of our aesthetic, but were part of the apartment. We're hoping to redo them when we have the time and money.

Proudest DIY

Turning a vanity closet, which was on offshoot of the main room, into a unique and useful sewing room and library.

Biggest Indulgence

We recently replaced our hand-me-down twenty-inch TV with a forty-inch, flat panel TV. We waited until we found a screen that could be mounted on the wall and blend in to our decor so much that many people say they didn't even notice it when they walked into the room.

Best Advice

Look at everything you own and imagine who among your friends might be best served by the item. If you yourself are truly best served by it, keep it. But if you can think of someone you know who could put it better to use, offer it to him or her.

Dream Source

On a trip to Paris, we visited the Clignancourt Flea Market and wished we had the money—and space—to pick up some of the wonderful pieces of furniture, accessories, toys, and art.

Emily added a piece of sustainable wood (far left) to the top of the bench she and Gregory found on Craigslist *and upholstered a cushion for it. They covered the floor in Sea Mist* Flor *tiles and painted the walls in Behr's Valley Mist. The* IKEA *desk is paired with an Eames chair purchased at the* Rose Bowl Flea Market. *The starburst patterns are created by sunlight on the curtains that Emily made from vintage fabric bought at* Sunset Orange.*

The bookcase (left) comes from Den of Antiquity *in Silverlake, and the wall-mounted fish bowl from* Post Modern Pets. *Gregory found the late 1950s wall clock on* eBay. *They painted the living room with* Benjamin Moore's *Bright Yellow. The couch and daybed are from the Case Study line by* Modernica. *They sourced the orange fiberglass ball chair at* Room Service *and the rug at* Target.*

The kitchen has changed little since the home was built. The stove and sink unit are original. The shelving above the stove comes from Kmart and the hanging basket from IKEA. Greg and Emily painted the walls Behr's Velvet Morning.

Greg and Emily painted their bedroom (opposite, top) Behr's Valley Mist. The bed frame is from the Case Study line by Modernica. The sheets are from Target. Emily made the curtains with fabric from ReproDepot and trim from MJtrim. Just above the headboard, they mounted a CD player from Muji.

Emily built a sewing room (above, left) into part of the large walk-in closet off the bedroom. The blue sewing machine, which inspired the room, came from her grandmother. The room is full of supplies tidily stored on shelves from Home Depot and Target and in pullout containers from IKEA and Zipper.

Both the bathroom walls and the bathtub (above, right) were painted Behr's Velvet Morning. The shadow boxes from Target display collectibles. Another box holds the toilet paper.

RESOURCES

BEHR: behr.com
BENJAMIN MOORE: benjaminmoore.com
CRAIGSLIST: craigslist.org
CRATE & BARREL: crateandbarrel.com
DEN OF ANTIQUITY: 323.665.1616
EBAY: ebay.com
FLOR: florcatalog.com
HOME DEPOT: homedepot.com
IKEA: ikea.com
KMART: kmart.com
MJTRIM: mjtrim.com
MODERNICA: modernica.net
MUJI: muji.net
POST MODERN PETS: postmodernpets.com
REPRODEPOT: reprodepotfabrics.com
ROOM SERVICE: roomservice-la.com
ROSE BOWL FLEA MARKET: rgcshows.com
SOUTHER SALAZAR: southersalazar.net
SUNSET ORANGE: 323.666.6898
TARGET: target.com
ZIPPER: zippergifts.com

photos by
jill
slater

14.

hakarl and jili's bold bright moves

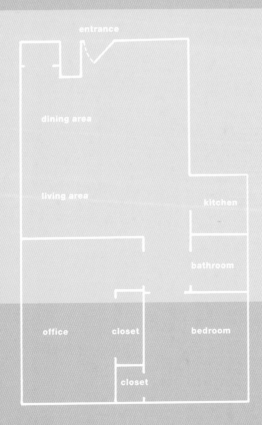

entrance

dining area

living area

kitchen

bathroom

office   closet   bedroom

closet

NAME: **HAKARL BEE** AND **JILI JIMENEZ**

PROFESSION: **CREATIVE DIRECTOR** (HAKARL)

AND FLORAL DESIGNER (JILI)

LOCATION: **WILLIAMSBURG, BROOKLYN**

OWNED/RENTED: **RENTED**

SIZE: **550 SQUARE FEET**

TYPE: **2-BEDROOM 4TH-FLOOR**

WALK-UP FROM THE EARLY 1990s

MONTHS LIVED IN: **6**

Have a rental and feel your hands are tied? Then this one is for you. Hakarl and Jili use color, bold graphics, and surprising scale choices to create a vibrant interior in an otherwise unexceptional rental. Their creativity, ingenuity, and attention to detail make it all work.

Let's talk about color first. Each room has one defining accent color that grabs your attention. A deep green greets you as you enter. A red lamp and sage green rug enliven the main room. Bright lime with stainless steel stands out in the kitchen. Paint is cheap, and Hakarl and Jili use it to prove that it's easy to make a high impact on a budget. In each room they have placed color on the wall that you see first. This effect frames your view. If you want to attempt this yourself, choose what we call the room's "show" wall – the one that you see when you enter.

Another trick that Hakarl and Jili use effectively is the placement of large objects among smaller ones. Every room has at least one element that another person might think is too big for the small apartment. Each serves to surprise and inspire – the huge graphic behind the sofa, the big chandelier in the hallway, the oversized paintings and mirror in the bedroom. Each creates visual flow as your eye moves between dissimilar objects.

In their previous apartment, Hakarl and Jili masked off floor-to-ceiling stripes on the walls before painting. Here, Hakarl took the approach one step further. He used tape to create the complex silhouette of a tree on one wall. The large mural is the focal point of the home. It's a stunningly simple and inexpensive idea that can easily be painted over when he and Jili choose to leave.

The large mural is the focal
point of the home.
It's a stunningly simple
and inexpensive idea that
can be easily painted over...

Hakarl and Jili bought the couch at a thrift store and the sheepskin throw at the Hell's Kitchen Flea Market. They found the coffee table on the street. To spruce up the ugly top and make it match the couch, Hakarl applied a strip of faux wood contact paper to the surface like a runner. He sealed the table edges with white contact paper. Believe it or not, even close up, it looks like wood veneer.

hakarl and jili's
survey

Style

A journey through twentieth-century pop culture.

Inspiration

The bones of our apartment as well as random finds in thrift stores and flea markets and on the street.

Favorite Element

The shell lamp in the entrance for its elegance (*Jili*). The beat-up stool in the living room (a hand-me-down from an old studio mate) for its many lives (*Hakarl*).

Biggest Challenge

Getting the two of us to agree on paint colors.

What Friends Say

Welcoming, cozy, and always good for inspiration.

Biggest Embarrassment

The doors—our landlord won't allow us to paint them.

Proudest DIY

Always the latest project—right now, the dining room crown molding with the fringe curtains.

Biggest Indulgence

The Design Within Reach couch in the office.

Best Advice

Get to know your space before you start furnishing.

Dream Sources

Thrift stores! Especially the ones on Seventeenth Street between Sixth and Seventh Avenues in Manhattan.

String window coverings (left) from Pearl River Mart, *used in the dining area, do not block the light, or obscure the view. Hakarl is high-concept, low-tech, so he attached the curtains using nails concealed behind the white molding at the top of the windows. He refers to the window treatment as "structured wallpaper."*

The wall unit (above), found at a West Seventeenth Street thrift store, is a large piece, one part of which is used here, in the living room. The other is in the office.

The pièce de résistance is the mural that Hakarl painted (left). To accomplish this feat, he first made a digital composite of trees that he projected on the living room wall. He then taped the edges of the pattern and cut it out. Finally, he painted within the taped lines with a black latex paint.

To spice up the rental kitchen (below), Hakarl painted the far wall green. For the other walls, he asked the local paint store to custom-mix a warm, neutral color. Hakarl then installed aluminum sheeting on the frame of each cabinet front and on the freezer door of the refrigerator. On the left wall hangs a piece of construction detritus from a salvage store in Williamsburg.

When Hakarl moved to the United States from Germany, the only family memento he brought with him in his suitcase was a teapot his mother received as a wedding gift forty years ago (below). He found the dining table on the street and the chairs at Las Venus. Hakarl bought the red lamp at Kawahara Design, the only place he could find the size he wanted. Inside it, Hakarl set an Edison bulb that goes on right before he comes home from work so the apartment feels "like someone has already been there."

To demarcate the dining area (top), Hakarl painted hardware-store molding white and cut it to fit the space above the windows closest to the dining table. You don't even notice that the molding doesn't appear elsewhere in the apartment.

Hakarl and Jili painted the entryway green (top and opposite) to separate it from the main space and make it feel like its own room. The wind chime from the Hell's Kitchen Flea Market satisfies Hakarl's love of bright, shiny objects. The chairs are part of a larger set that Hakarl found at one of the many used furniture stores along West Seventeenth Street in Manhattan.

Hakarl loves lamps, but Jili makes him edit his collection once in a while, so this lamp (above, left) is on the way out.

The mirrors are from closet doors. In the bedroom (above, right), mirrors (also from closet doors) serve as a headboard.

Hakarl framed prints that he found at the Seventeenth
Street Flea Market. *Antlers purchased on* eBay *from a
Canadian rancher are displayed in a vessel from* Housing
Works *thrift shop.*

*Hakarl and Jili are lucky enough to have a second bedroom that
they use as a guest room and office. The couch, from* Design
Within Reach, *flips out to become a bed. They paid ten dollars for the large overhanging lamp at the* Hell's Kitchen Flea
Market *because it lacked a base. Hakarl later found a large um-
brella base on the street that worked perfectly. The desk, big
enough for two, is an old dining table.*

RESOURCES

DESIGN WITHIN REACH: dwr.com

EBAY: ebay.com

HELL'S KITCHEN FLEA MARKET: hellskitchenfleamarket.com

HOUSING WORKS: housingworks.org

KAWAHARA DESIGN: 212.736.5858

LAS VENUS: lasvenus.com

PEARL RIVER MART: pearlriver.com

photos by
jill slater

15.
ivar's pared down and simple

bathroom

closet

closet

entrance

kitchen

closet

office area

bedroom area

living area

NAME: IVAR RAPHAEL
PROFESSION: WOODWORKER
LOCATION: UPPER WEST SIDE, NYC
OWNED/RENTED: OWNED
SIZE: 325 SQUARE FEET
TYPE: STUDIO IN A GUSTAVINO 5-STORY
BROWNSTONE BUILT IN 1886
YEARS LIVED IN: 5

When we first saw Ivar's apartment, we knew we had found a soul mate.

Possibly the most spartan apartment we have ever seen, it proved our long-held belief that a few beautiful pieces of art or furniture are preferable to a roomful of random stuff.

Ivar has the advantage of living alone – his apartment has to accommodate only one person's things – but the more we looked around, the more we realized that Ivar has taken minimalism to an extreme. He has very few belongings, and what little he has is stored behind closed doors. With everything out of sight, the small studio seems spacious and calm. His apartment boasts French doors with a full Juliet balcony, which adds light and contributes to the feeling of spaciousness. The apartment, though small, has a built-in romantic design.

Creating what Ivar calls a "contemplative space" is possible in any home as long as you are disciplined. His approach is all about editing and stripping down to essentials. Ivar reminds us of Antoine de Saint-Exupéry, who said, "In anything at all, perfection is finally attained not when there is no longer anything to add, but when there is no longer anything to take away, when a body has been stripped down to its nakedness."

Ivar has certainly stripped his home down to its nakedness: he has one bed, two tables, and three chairs, along with a generous amount of original artwork. To achieve this level of minimalism, Ivar has let go of many things that others might have *had* to keep. We promise that Ivar has no big storage closet somewhere else in the city or at his parents' house. This really is all he owns.

Ivar made the lounge chair (far left) from walnut that a tree-surgeon friend felled in New Jersey and bought from its owners. He stained it with four coats of varnish.

Each piece in Ivar's apartment has a specific origin. He made the bowls (left), his earliest pieces, with curly maple and beech from park trees felled in a New Jersey neighborhood.

ivar's
survey

Style

Postindustrial craft.

Inspiration

Having lived in cluttered spaces, I wanted my first apartment to be a contemplative space that embraced art and design in a simple and selective way. Extensive use of lighting creates a pleasant mood that is further enhanced by art. The furniture and wood sculptures are all self-made, and the white walls serve as a neutral palette for meditation on their design.

Favorite Element

The Juliet balcony.

Biggest Challenge

Blending disparate elements while avoiding decoration clichés.

What Friends Say

Aside from an ex-girlfriend who called the kitchen cold and impersonal, most people respond favorably.

Biggest Embarrassment

The bathroom is in need of renovation.

Proudest DIY

All the wood furniture and bowls.

Biggest Indulgence

The custom-made balcony French doors.

Best Advice

William Morris said, "Have nothing in your house that you do not know to be useful or believe to be beautiful."

Dream Source

The Pier Antiques Show on the West Side of Manhattan.

When Ivar moved in, he couldn't afford the furniture he really liked, so he started making himself one piece at a time. He found additional pieces on eBay and at the Brimfield Flea Market. Ivar's cousin made the mobile, and his father did the painting. Ivar made the pedestal from a salvaged redwood fence post.

In the sleeping area (opposite), Ivar put a Home Depot drop cloth over a mattress with pillows from his mother. He says that he feels "fabric-challenged," so he went for *the cheapest option in the most natural color possible. The wall behind the bed was originally exposed brick. He covered it with drywall because he felt the brick was inappropriate for a Victorian brownstone. The light next to the bed is an O. C. White lamp anchored to a base that Ivar made by turning maple on a lathe. He rewired this lamp and others using Sundial Wire, purchased online, which looks like twisted rope and approximates the original wiring.*

"Have nothing in your house
that you do not know
to be useful or believe to be
beautiful." —william morris

Ivar's design for the elm bookshelf (opposite, top left) was inspired by curtain wall architecture, where the supports are not in the corners, and by cabinets that have glass on the ends or corners.

The large painting (opposite, top left) is by his father, and the nineteenth-century landscapes (left) are from the Hell's Kitchen Flea Market *and the* Golden Nugget Flea Market. *The bird atop the small painting (opposite, top right) is a shooting gallery target from Flint, Michigan, that Ivar found on* eBay.

(opposite, bottom) The high ceilings accommodate these great cabinets that Ivar purchased off the shelf at Home Depot. General Sheet Metal Works *fabricated the stainless steel counter and shaped it to the plywood base and backsplash. The undercounter refrigerator is a* Kenmore *from* Sears, *and the stove is by* Avanti. *Ivar created the light on the counter by putting an* Aerolux bulb *from* eBay *inside a small flowerpot.*

The American black walnut Parsons table serves as Ivar's desk. The chair is made from the same tree as the desk. The lamp (above right), designed to be carried in a toolbox, folds in on itself to protect the bulb. Ivar found it at the Hell's Kitchen Flea Market.

RESOURCES

AVANTI: avantiproducts.com

BRIMFIELD FLEA MARKET:

journalofantiques.com/briminfo.htm

EBAY: ebay.com

GENERAL SHEET METAL WORKS: generalsheetmetalworks.com

GOLDEN NUGGET FLEA MARKET: gnmarket.com

HELL'S KITCHEN FLEA MARKET: hellskitchenfleamarket.com

HOME DEPOT: homedepot.com

LAMBERTVILLE ANTIQUE FLEA MARKET:

keysfleamarket.com/fleamarket/state/new_jersey.htm

SEARS: sears.com

SUNDIAL WIRE: sundialwire.com

james vira

16.
james and margaret's iconic studio

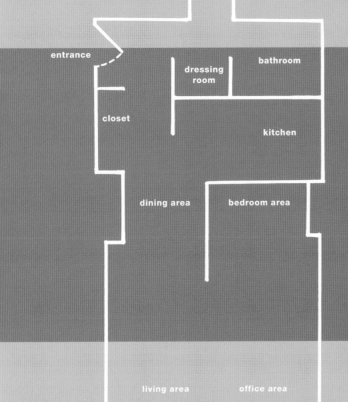

entrance

dressing room

bathroom

closet

kitchen

dining area

bedroom area

living area

office area

NAME: JAMES AND MARGARET VIRA
PROFESSION: ARCHITECTS
LOCATION: KIPS BAY, MANHATTAN, NYC
OWNED/RENTED: OWNED
SIZE: 565 SQUARE FEET
TYPE: STUDIO IN A 1961 HIGH-RISE
YEARS LIVED IN: 4.5

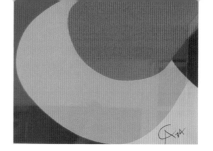

This home shows you how smart architects can be.

James and Margaret's studio apartment would have put off most prospective buyers with a baby on the way. The studio had an unstructured, unworkable floor plan and poor storage and was too small for most families of three. James and Margaret, however, were drawn to Kips Bay Towers, designed by icon I. M. Pei, and saw a way the apartment could work for them.

James and Margaret began by redrawing the floor plan and gutting half of the apartment. They then transformed the space with their own vision. The new apartment is still an open studio, but now it has four different "rooms," each offering a sense of privacy. If you're tempted to put up walls to create a new room and make more space, take a look at this studio first. The main feature is a wood wall that strongly sections the space and provides for multiple functions. It is also a fantastic visual design element.

In spite of the complexity and expense of redesigning an apartment, there is something straightforward and approachable in the way James and Margaret have done it. After touring their home, you may decide to ramp up your next DIY project.

(previous page) James and Margaret were limited by finances, so the process of finishing the apartment took a long time. Over the course of a year and a half, James worked on the wall during lunch breaks and in the evening. They cut the wall frame with a router out of multiple pieces of plywood, which allowed him to create the subtle curves and hard angles that you see. He and Margaret then placed walnut slats over the plywood frame. The overhang creates an intimate dining space and also provided a convenient way to install the pendant lights in the ceiling. *The bench in the dining area contains storage space that extends through the wall into the bedroom.*

The storage under the dining area bench provides bookshelf space for the bedroom (right and opposite). The Ella bed is from Room and Board. *James and Margaret designed the nightstands, which are built into the wall. The light is part of the Aloha Series from* Rejuvenation. *The couple sanded the original oak floor and stained it with a mix of Jacobean and Walnut* Minwax.

james and margaret's
survey

Style
Livable modern.

Inspiration
The I. M. Pei–designed building with its floor-to-ceiling windows and view.

Favorite Element
The walnut wood divider wall that creates dining, sleeping, and storage areas.

Biggest Challenge
Organizing the plan so three people could comfortably cohabitate, without creating a series of enclosed rooms.

What Friends Say
People of varying design tastes love the simplicity of the overall design and the ingenuity of the multifunctional wood wall.

Biggest Embarrassment
Not having the finances to redo the bathroom.

Proudest DIY
Each board in the wood wall was individually cut to size and arranged on the framing with regard to both color and grain pattern for a well-balanced and variegated composition.

Biggest Indulgence
Splurging on solid walnut boards rather than using veneered plywood.

Best Advice
If it's worth doing, it's worth doing right. Always assume things are going to take longer than you think they will.

Dream Sources
Rockler, Custom Cabinets Plus, Nemo Tile, Overstock.com, Retromodern.com.

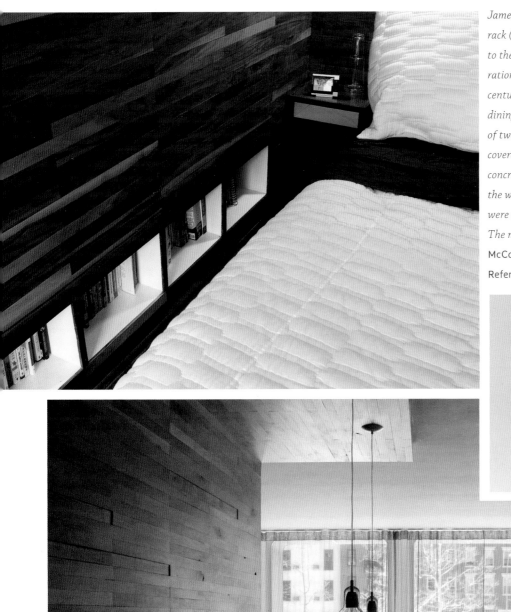

James designed and built the vertical wine rack (below) out of walnut. It was a precursor to the wall project but is clearly of similar inspiration. James and Margaret found the mid-century credenza on **eBay** and designed their dining table (below, bottom). The top consists of two layers of plywood glued together and covered with **Rockite** – a fast-setting, pourable concrete – which provides a thin covering atop the wood and fills the gaps. The wood squares were then colored in varying shades of black. The metal base came from **Rockler**. The **Paul McCobb** chairs were an **eBay** find. The **Sophie Refer bulb lights** are from **Ameico**.

James and Margaret designed the kitchen and hired contractors to build it. They chose blue cabinets with a white Corian counter, and an energy-efficient ConServ refrigerator. The flooring is original. The artwork is Herman Miller's *Summer Picnic* series, which James inherited from his former architecture firm. The George Nelson *clock* is from eBay.

The couple painted the kitchen walls with Pratt and Lambert's *Tobacco* and installed track lighting from Home Depot.

The backsplash is made of blue ceramic penny tiles from Nemo Tile.

The Marcel Breuer *table was later replaced by a baby crib. The* BluDot *desk is from* Overstock.com. *The* Eames *aluminum group chair was purchased on eBay. The painting is by Robert Szot.*

James and Margaret found the rug on Overstock .com. The couch is a Florence Knoll knockoff from Claank Design. James built the TV stand out of plywood and steel rods. The curtains were custom-made from Knoll Silver Screen fabric. The fabric, 100 percent polyester and printed on one side with a thin aluminum coating, reflects the sun and ensures privacy for the first-floor apartment.

RESOURCES

AMEICO: ameico.com

BLUDOT: bludot.com

CLAANK DESIGN: claank.com

CONSERV: conservrefrigerators.com

CUSTOM CABINETS PLUS: customcabinetsplus.com

EBAY: ebay.com

HOME DEPOT: homedepot.com

KNOLL: knoll.com

NEMO TILE: nemotile.com

OVERSTOCK.COM: overstock.com

PRATT AND LAMBERT: prattandlambert.com

REJUVENATION: rejuvenation.com

ROCKITE: rockite.com

ROCKLER: rockler.com

ROOM AND BOARD: roomandboard.com

photos by
jill slater

17.

jane and darko's cozy thicket

bedroom

closet

kitchen

entrance

bathroom

office area

dining area   living area

NAME: JANE MOUNT AND DARKO KARAS
PROFESSION: OWNERS AND OPERATORS
OF LOADBEARING, A SWISS
FURNITURE IMPORTER
LOCATION: EAST VILLAGE, NYC
OWNED/RENTED: OWNED
SIZE: 645 SQUARE FEET
TYPE: 1-BEDROOM IN A 5-STORY
BUILDING FROM THE LATE 1800s
YEARS LIVED IN: 1

It's rare to find people who can cram a lot into an apartment and still make it feel open and comfortable. Jane and Darko own a railroad apartment and a ton of possessions — Jane is a collector — but have managed to organize their space so that it's colorful and funky, and totally welcoming.

You enter directly into the living/dining area and immediately see two supersmart uses of space: a full-wall bookcase with a window seat and a sofa and dining table arranged to split the room. Most of us would have pushed the sofa against a wall and never considered a long banquet table for such a small space. But the sofa makes one room work as two, and the long table adds a surprising element of scale that suggests the room is larger than it is.

Darko created the layout using his 3-D animation expertise. He first made a rendering of the entire apartment, then experimented with different furniture and colors. The program allowed him to "fly through" the apartment at a slow speed to see how it all worked. The apartment spreads itself out into four distinct areas: living/dining room, office, kitchen, and bedroom at the back. Each has a different design scheme, which creates a side-to-side flow that breaks up the long hallway connecting all the areas.

One of the most interesting aspects is Jane and Darko's concept of being in the woods. Their nature-inspired aesthetic is expressed through an element in each room. They papered a kitchen wall with leafless birch trees, made a shower curtain out of Tord Boontje's dreamy starscape, and on facing bedroom walls contrasted a bear and a full-color forest that reminds us of 1970s hotel rooms.

The overall effect is fresh and lively, with bold colors, ornate lighting fixtures, and a carefully orchestrated, eclectic mix of furniture. Welcome to an urban refuge and a home full of wonder.

ON FACING BEDROOM WALLS...
A BEAR AND A FULL-COLOR FOREST
THAT REMINDS US OF 1970s
HOTEL ROOMS.

jane and darko's
survey

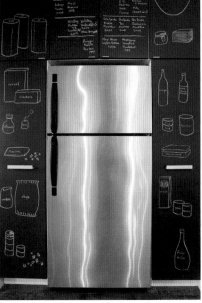

Style

Clean, modern sense of design with a quirky, artsy sense of humor. Our space is efficient, usable, and practical but with a sense of magic and wonder throughout.

Inspiration

We were inspired by thickets—intimate but slightly wild and magical spaces of refuge in forests. We spend all day working in Manhattan, surrounded by concrete and metal and people, and we want to feel the opposite after the day is over.

Favorite Element

Besides the flat-screen TV, of course, the wall of bookshelves we built at the end of the living room (*Darko*). Having the space for our growing collection of mini-art (*Jane*).

Biggest Challenge

Darko, being Swiss, owns only a pocket knife and a watch, but Jane is a collector. The challenge was to find ways to store all of our necessary clothing, books, and other things without making such a small space feel cluttered.

What Friends Say

We feel flattered when it's 3:30 A.M. after a dinner party and the last guests are just on their way out the door because they don't want to leave. Some of our friends feel it's a place they love to visit but can't imagine living in, and some wish they could move right in.

Biggest Embarrassment

The tumbleweeds of cat hair that somehow always collect under the sofa despite our best cleaning efforts.

Proudest DIY

Our bedroom closets with the forest view made from IKEA cabinets and a picture we took upstate.

Biggest Indulgences

We have two big indulgences, one useful and one purely aesthetic. The useful one is the Viking stove. It's small for a Viking, only thirty inches wide, but it's perfect. The aesthetic indulgence was the skim-coating of the walls. Neither of us really believed skim-coating was necessary or would make a real difference, but Jane's mother convinced us it would be worth having it done, and she was right.

Best Advice

A friend who had remodeled his apartment told us to find a good contractor for the big projects, and that it was worth paying a little more for excellent work so that we wouldn't have to hire someone later to fix the mess left by a cheaper contractor.

Dream Sources

Our dream is a great piece at a bargain, usually online. We found great stuff at Ylighting.com and Retromodern.com and even big retailers like HomeDepot.com.

Jane and Darko put in Home Depot's unpolished black granite countertops (opposite top right). They debated between white marble and black granite – the latter was cheaper and stains less. The IKEA Akurum cabinets have a high-lacquer finish called Abstrakt. The sink is from Home Depot and has a Hans Grohe faucet. The shelving above the sink was built by a contractor they praise highly, Dutchman Contracting. A counter-length piece of glass protects the wallpaper between the upper and lower cabinets. The wallpaper is Woods by Cole and Son. The Agave light fixture from Luceplan comes with changeable red, blue, and yellow filters. The vintage French desk and old work stool are from B4 It Was Cool. A metalworker extended the legs so the desk could be used as the kitchen island.

On one kitchen wall, Jane and Darko installed IKEA's cheapest cabinets in the Akurum line and painted them with two coats of chalkboard paint (opposite, bottom). The drawings illustrate what is inside the cabinets. The cabinets above the refrigerator hold their wine collection.

The divider (right, top), a Case Study piece from Modernica, holds glassware and candles and creates separation between the office and the dining area. The stenographer's desk is from a vintage furniture store in Switzerland. The chair is a Non chair from Conran.

Jane designed the built-in shelves (above) with a lot of help from her mother. The brick wall was already exposed. Jane and Darko stained the floors using Minwax's English Chestnut. The extralarge strut table is from BluDot, and the Murano glass chandelier is from ABC Carpet & Home.

The media console (below) is from the Case Study series from Moder-nica. Jane's father had the two Plexiglas tables made thirty years ago. The Turkish woven fish rug is from **ABC Carpet & Home**. The Bourgie lamp is from **Kartell**. Next to it is artwork by **Howard Finster** and **Patrick Earl Barnes**. Jane had the chair from **Anthropologie** reuphol-stered to give it a 1920s French look. The walls are painted Atlantic Winter by **Benjamin Moore**.

(opposite, top) Jane and Darko based the redesign of the apartment on how much space the bedroom needed in order to accommodate a king-sized bed. The walnut bed is from Switzerland. The wool shag carpet is a remnant from **ABC Carpet & Home**. They painted the walls **Benjamin Moore's** Silver Fox. Jane painted the piece above the bed.

(opposite, bottom) Jane and Darko needed more storage in the bedroom than the walk-in closet provided, so they installed four **IKEA** Pax cabi-nets. To decorate them, they had a photo that they took printed on wallpaper at **GalleryStreet.com** and cov-ered the cabinets as well as some of the wall to their left. The **Luceplan Blow** ceiling fan is from **Ylighting.com**, and the track lighting is from **Home Depot**.

(opposite, top) The 1940s yellow chair by a French designer, from **R20th Century,** *is more for display than seating.*

(opposite, bottom) Unable to find an affordable and appealing console for the bathroom sink, Jane and Darko made one. They bought an unfinished wood desk, sawed it in half, sprayed it with high-gloss black paint, and cut a hole in the top. The sink is **Porcher**'s Como *and the faucet is by* **Starck** *for* **Hans Grohe.** Tod Boontje's *Until Dawn curtain hangs outside the shower liner.*

This lantern-slide catalog (above), purchased at the **Hell's Kitchen Flea Market,** *sits in the hallway. Some drawers still contained slides of the work of the artist who sold it to them. Jane and Darko added their collection of small objects, which stays out of sight until someone is curious enough to open a drawer.*

RESOURCES

ABC CARPET & HOME: abchome.com

ANTHROPOLOGIE: anthropologie.com

B4 IT WAS COOL: 212.219.0139

BENJAMIN MOORE: benjaminmoore.com

BLUDOT: bludot.com

COLE AND SON: cole-and-son.com

CONRAN: conran.com

DUTCHMAN CONTRACTING: dutchmancontracting.com

GALLERYSTREET.COM: gallerystreet.com

HANS GROHE: hansgrohe.com

HELL'S KITCHEN FLEA MARKET: hellskitchenfleamarket.com

HOME DEPOT: homedepot.com

IKEA: ikea.com

KARTELL: kartell.com

LUCEPLAN: luceplan.com

MODERNICA: modernica.net

PORCHER: porcher-us.com

R20TH CENTURY: r20thcentury.com

VIKING: vikingrange.com

YLIGHTING.COM: ylighting.com

photos by
jill slater

18.
jenny and clove's
LA-ish studio

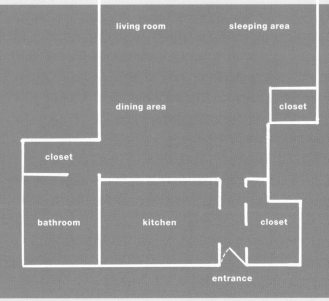

living room   sleeping area

dining area   closet

closet

bathroom   kitchen   closet

entrance

NAME: **JENNY** AND **CLOVE**
PROFESSION: **VIDEO ARTIST** (JENNY)
AND **CHOREOGRAPHER** (CLOVE)
LOCATION: **ASTOR PLACE, NYC**
OWNED/RENTED: **OWNED**
SIZE: **442 SQUARE FEET**
TYPE: **GROUND-FLOOR STUDIO IN
A LARGE 1940s CO-OP COMPLEX**
YEARS LIVED IN: **1.5**

*Jenny and Clove's need for efficiency never overshadows
their desire for elegance and style. Jenny found the two* Milo
Baughman *chairs (right) on* Craigslist. *The lamp in front of
the window is by* Martha Stewart.

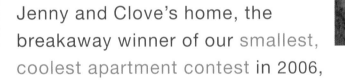

Jenny and Clove's home, the breakaway winner of our smallest, coolest apartment contest in 2006,

is an awesome example of how to create a gem out of what on first sight looked like a dung heap. Twelve cats had previously lived in the studio. The walls were covered with forty-five years' worth of nicotine, and the place had no appliances. In addition, the apartment is below ground level and faces the rear of the building. Although the studio would have put off many prospective buyers, Jenny and Clove saw hidden potential.

Jenny and Clove had renovated their first shared home, a Victorian formerly lived in by Jack London, in Oakland, California. They missed the Bay Area indoor/outdoor life-style, so when they saw the wall of casement windows leading from the interior of the apartment to the garden, they flipped out. This extra square footage would allow them to incorporate elements of their previous life in California and expand their sense of home.

To achieve the spacious feeling they wanted, they had to set priorities. The apartment would be primarily for working, relaxing, and entertaining, and secondarily for sleeping. Using a Murphy bed helps give the space the feeling of an expansive (and expensive) loft, allowing them to host, they say, a "ten-person dinner, a fifteen-person salon, or a two-hundred-person raging party!"

With near-military precision, Jenny scoured Craigslist for furnishings. She was amazed at the quality of New York's Craigslist and used it to create a sleek, modern studio space that integrates natural elements reflecting Bay Area influences. The control that Jenny and Clove exercised in the renovation process allowed them to focus on the smallest details, creating design "moments" on a level with a custom, high-end home.

jenny and clove's
survey

Style

Midcentury modern meets California bohemian.

Inspiration

Joseph Eichler, the elements, modern Japanese design, and California indoor/outdoor style.

Favorite Elements

The wall of casement windows (*Jenny*), the exposed salvaged raw timbers in the kitchen (*Clove*), and the private garden that doubles the size of the apartment.

Biggest Challenge

Removing two kitchen walls and then moving and rerouting all the plumbing, gas, and electrical.

What Friends Say

Beautiful and incredibly quiet. No one can believe we live in New York City.

Biggest Embarrassment

That it doesn't have a separate bedroom and folks always assume it does.

Proudest DIY Project

Rehabilitating the casement windows. There were at least forty years of rust on them.

Biggest Indulgence

Our dishwasher (it is a marriage saver) and our refrigerator (because we go on tour so often, we had to have the manual defrost).

Best Advice

Our building's handyman suggested that we put our track lighting on a wireless switch available at RadioShack for supercheap. That part of the room doesn't have wiring for overhead lights. The remote allows us to turn the lights on and off effortlessly. The only issue is that it doesn't offer a dimmer option.

Dream Source

New York Craigslist; it is unlike anything we've ever seen.

(opposite) Jenny has a knack for finding high-end furnishings in great condition on Craigslist. That was the source for the Ligne Roset sectional couch and the cowhide rug (originally from Evolution). The coffee table, consisting of two glass cubes, was on sale at Crate & Barrel.

The windows and door frames (above, top left) were covered with decades of paint layers and rust. For one full week, Jenny and Clove stripped the paint to reach the beautiful steel frames.

The Zeus White Silestone counters (above, bottom left) and the Verona cooktop and oven are from Home Depot. The extradeep Kindred sink from homecenter.com has a Bagvik chrome faucet from IKEA. The brushed aluminum handles are from Home Depot. The dishwasher is a Miele Slimline.

The vintage fabric panel (above, right) from Repro Depot conceals a Murphy bed. The wall of bookshelves looks built-in but is made of freestanding units.

the need for efficiency never overshadows the desire for elegance and style.

Rather than use the customary materials to reframe the kitchen (above), Jenny chose more aesthetically pleasing salvaged timbers from M. Fine Lumber *of Brooklyn. She feels that they have a lot of character and "enhance the room with a Zen-temple flair." Jenny and Clove indulged in the luxury of a tall, narrow* Liebherr *refrigerator. They installed* IKEA Abstrakt *white base cabinets. The upper cabinets have Avsikt frosted glass doors. The lights in the cabinets are also from* IKEA. *The recessed lighting is from* Home Depot.

All three closet units (right) come from California Closets.

The barn-wood dining table is huge, in theory, for a studio apartment, but here it feels like a natural fit. It can easily seat eight for a cozy dinner party. Jenny and Clove bought the Olde Goode Things table secondhand at a West Village sidewalk sale. Jenny found the four McCobb stools on Craigslist. They invented a floor stain to mask the cat damage from the previous tenant's tenure: a mix of Minwax Ebony and Jacobean applied thickly and left on for two days.

The office space has a huge desk and a chair from Jenny's grad school days. The lamp is from Pottery Barn. The TV stand is from Design Within Reach. Jenny and Clove used twelve coats of primer on the walls (Jenny recommends Gripper by Glidden) to keep the previous tenants' nicotine build-up at bay. The colors they chose, all by Benjamin Moore, include Ice Mist, Sea Foam, Ocean Air, Gossamer Blue, and Super White.

RESOU

BENJAMIN MOORE: benjaminmoore.com

CALIFORNIA CLOSETS: californiaclosets.com

CRAIGSLIST: craigslist.org

CRATE & BARREL: crateandbarrel.com

DESIGN WITHIN REACH: dwr.com

EVOLUTION: theevolutionstore.com

HOME CENTER: homecenter.com

HOME DEPOT: homedepot.com

IKEA: ikea.com

LIEBHERR: liebherr.com/lh/en

LIGNE ROSET: ligne-roset-usa.com

MARTHA STEWART: marthastewart.com

M. FINE LUMBER: mfinelumber.com

MIELE: miele.com

OLDE GOODE THINGS: oldegoodthings.com

POTTERY BARN: potterybarn.com

RADIOSHACK: radioshack.com

REPRO DEPOT: reprodepot.com

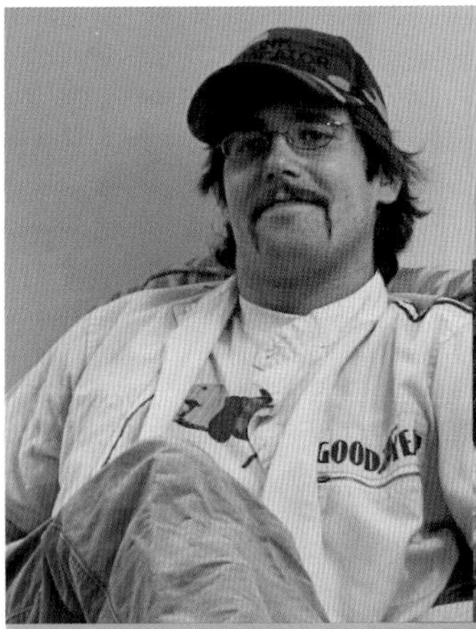

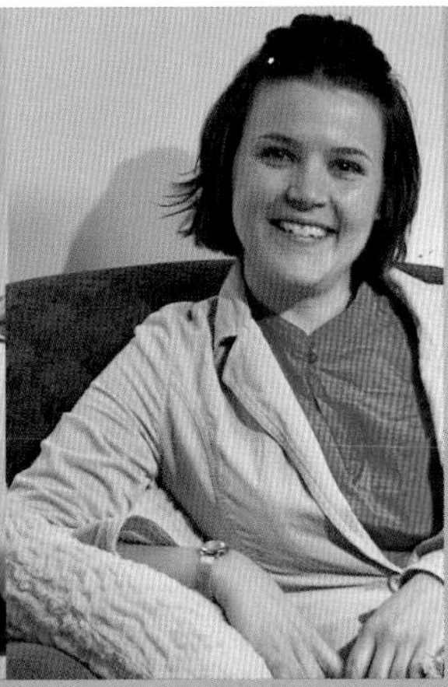

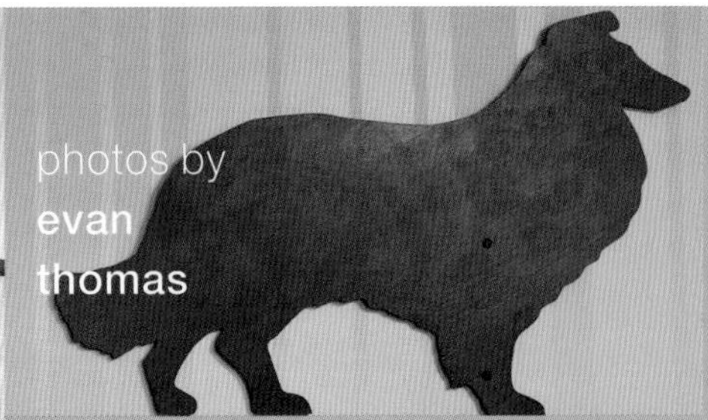

photos by
evan
thomas

19.

jessica and andrius, artists in residence

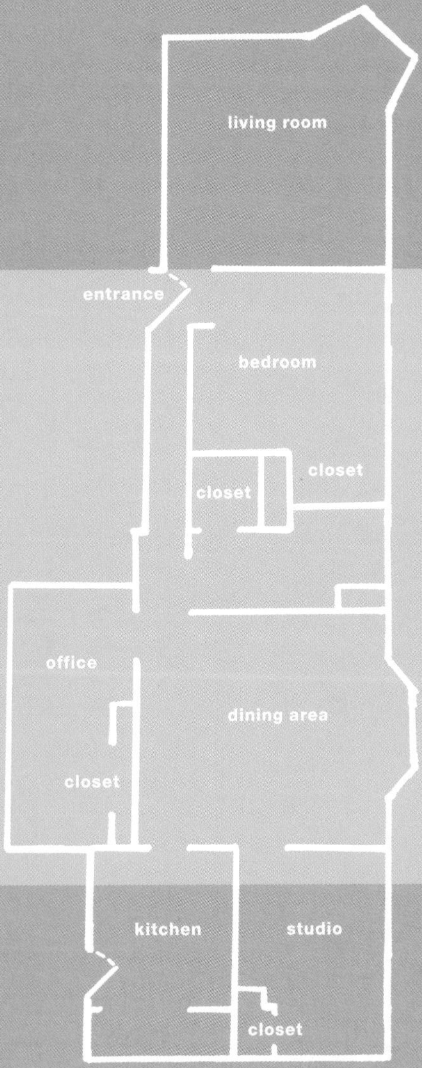

living room
entrance
bedroom
closet
closet
office
dining area
closet
kitchen
studio
closet

NAME: JESSICA BARTLETT AND ANDRIUS JUTZI
PROFESSION: GIFT COORDINATOR AT NORTHWESTERN UNIVERSITY LIBRARY AND COEDITOR OF DESIGNBONER.COM (JESSICA) AND FREELANCE ARTIST (ANDRIUS)
LOCATION: UPTOWN, CHICAGO
OWNED/RENTED: OWNED
SIZE: 1,200 SQUARE FEET
TYPE: 3-BEDROOM CONDO IN CIRCA-1902 BUILDING
YEARS LIVED IN: 2.5 YEARS

experimentation
and energy pulse me.

The bathroom renovation was a big project for Andrius, but the results look professional. He chose the wall and floor tiles at Tile Outlet and sourced vintage fixtures. Jessica got the handmade toilet seat cover at the Renegade Craft Fair. The "Love Lights" switch plate is one of her own creations.

As you tour Jessica and Andrius's home, you will find that each room is completely different from the previous one. Unusual design ideas abound. The living room boasts vertical stripes of alternating widths, painted the same color but in different finishes, topped off with a bold chocolate brown horizontal stripe. The handmade window treatment consists of coffee-stained vellum sheets framed with thin black balsa strips. Resembling old milk glass, the panels provide the privacy needed for this garden-level apartment without sacrificing natural light.

Experimentation and energy pulse through their home. Jessica and Andrius did not know exactly what each room would eventually look like when they moved in. Nor did they worry about matching all of their furniture. Instead, they tried different things in different rooms, enjoyed a few failures along the way, and always allowed the room itself to dictate the process. The results are much livelier than anything you'll find in a staged, shelter-mag design.

Their talent for redesign and making things work extends to their furnishings. Only four items were purchased brand-new. Jessica scored some amazing pieces from a library where she worked. Andrius loves the vintage stereo system (it works perfectly!) that he listened to as a kid at his grandmother's house.

Amid all this creativity, you'll also find discipline. They flawlessly carried out every idea—including the partially removed wallpaper. Such conviction makes any interior successful. You can be eclectic and you can work with found objects, *and* you can change styles from room to room, but this will work only if, like Jessica and Andrius, you go whole hog.

Andrius painted the living room (opposite, top) in alternating glossy and flat stripes of **Benjamin Moore** Antique White, topped with a dark brown border. The window treatments are made from coffee-stained vellum sheets framed with black-painted balsa wood, which is sturdy enough to provide structure and prevent warping. The valances are foam-wrapped MDF panels covered in canvas. Bifold doors and hardware from **Home Depot** were used to build the bookshelves.

Andrius painted the hallway (opposite, bottom left) with a custom color mix. A bench from Jessica's grandfather holds pillows from the **Pillow Dreams Project**. Andrius's frame collection and antlers from his great-uncle decorate the walls.

The vibrant glass vessels (opposite, bottom right) look beautiful and also function as a privacy screen for the garden-level window. The cowboy was Jessica's first **eBay** purchase.

The dining room (above) is painted with a custom blend that Jessica describes as "ivory, rosy red, and Pepto-Bismol pink with an ocher glaze." Jessica inherited the dining table from her grandfather and the book and record storage pieces from a library where she once worked. A painting by **Katie Brown** hangs next to an alley find — the supersized orange glass lamp. The couple's studio is through the doorway.

The office walls (left) have a DIY suede-textured finish inspired by **Ralph Lauren** suede paint but executed for a fraction of the cost. First, a coat of dark blue paint was rolled on the walls. Then Andrius added a bit of white to the blue and brushed on the lighter paint with X strokes, allowing some of the original color to show through. Craft supplies are stored in wine and fruit crates. The eagle lamp on the side table is from a garage sale, and the oval mirror is from the **Salvation Army**. The sofa is an **IKEA** purchase.

jessica and andrius's
survey

Style

Blended. We don't adhere to one style. Both of us definitely like old stuff. We love finding unique and, oftentimes, worn furniture at thrift stores and garage sales, and even in alleys.

Inspiration

Freedom! This is our first non-rented space, and we're living it up in terms of design and experimentation.

Favorite Element

Andrius's new favorite spot is the "knitting nook" in the living room. The oddly shaped bay window space had stumped us for a long time. By putting the chair there, adding the floor lamp, and directing everything slightly away from the TV, it becomes a cozy, separate space.

Biggest Challenge

Lighting. We live in a garden-unit condo now, so lighting is especially tricky. We need to get better at accent lighting, working with lamps, dimmers, and various types of window treatments. We rely too heavily on natural light and the dreaded overhead.

What Friends Say

"Wow!" The wall colors are a shocker to a lot of people. Some people have told us that our place reminds them of a museum in that there's always something new to see. The most common reaction we get is surprise at the amount of space that we have.

Biggest Embarrassment

The kitchen. It's teeny-tiny, slightly awkward, and a total collision of random building materials. It's the only room we haven't quite figured out yet.

Proudest DIY

Our window treatments in the living room. We love the morning light that we get through this set of three windows and wanted to keep as much of that as possible.

Biggest Indulgence

Color. Andrius is a painter, and his skills get utilized to their apex in our house. Many of our wall colors are custom blends.

Best Advice

Hire a plumber to do the plumbing. Handymen are great for certain things, but when it comes to the pipes, find a professional. We've lived through enough soggy encounters to learn that one shouldn't skimp on the waterways.

Dream Source

Auctions, estate sales, and generally any store that sells furniture for more than $200 per piece.

The bedside lamp from the **Salvation Army** *echoes the bedposts. The garage-sale bamboo shade on the window is softened by Jessica's first sewing project, a simple panel curtain.*

New furnishings fit comfortably with the vintage pieces. The twin orange glass lamps (above) are from **Target**, and the large white pitcher is from **West Elm**. The circa-1900 dental chair came from a prop sale held on the set of a TV show where Andrius worked. Jessica bought the mirror at an antique shop in Massachusetts. The dining table centerpiece is a large collection of markers.

Jessica and Andrius planned to strip the wallpaper (right) from the bedroom walls before painting. Partway through the job, they thought that the colors and textures looked beautiful, so they stopped. The patterned wall suits the bedroom's retro feel. The romance-novel switch plate pairs well with the old-fashioned wallpaper. The spray-painted stencil family portraits are by Jessica's sister, Alison.

RESOURCES

ANDRIUS JUTZI:
designboner.blogspot.com

BENJAMIN MOORE:
benjaminmoore.com

EBAY: ebay.com

HOME DEPOT: homedepot.com

IKEA: ikea.com

KATIE BROWN:
kfreshpaintings.com

PILLOW DREAMS PROJECT:
pillowdreamsproject.com

RENEGADE CRAFT FAIR:
renegadecraft.com

SALVATION ARMY: salvationarmyusa.org

TARGET: target.com

TILE OUTLET: 773.276.2662

WEST ELM: westelm.com

photos by
jill slater

20.
jill's DIY laboratory

Floor plan labels: office area · closet · stage · bathroom · dining area · bedroom · kitchen · living area · closet · entrance

NAME: JILL SLATER
PROFESSION: WRITER AND EDITOR
LOCATION: FINANCIAL DISTRICT, NYC
OWNED/RENTED: OWNED
SIZE: 610 SQUARE FEET
TYPE: STUDIO IN A 1907 INDUSTRIAL/OFFICE BUILDING CONVERTED TO RESIDENTIAL IN THE EARLY 1980s
YEARS LIVED IN: 2

The shelf along the perimeter of Jill's upstairs bedroom (opposite) holds her vast collection of dried plant materials, arranged on old military cafeteria trays. The far wall displays collages, found art, paintings, prints, and framed posters. Each work is individually attached to monofilament and hangs from an aluminum strip anchored to the wall about a foot below the ceiling. The truck image on the floor leaning against the wall is a traffic sign from a small town in eastern Slovakia. The two Communist posters on the left wall are from a junk shop in Sofia, Bulgaria.

Jill put many years of passionate thought, work, and problem solving into her space,

whether she was living in New York or in places as varied as San Francisco and the Czech Republic. When she bought this apartment, it was a blank slate. Over time, she systematically gutted and renovated the space, carrying out much of the demolition with her own bare hands. She did so much research that she's a walking encyclopedia of knowledge about materials, stores, and appliances.

Jill's inventiveness is on display throughout the apartment. She created an upstairs bedroom that takes advantage of the high ceilings. For the downstairs living area, she designed a clever stage that leaves the space open while providing storage. To plan the kitchen, she used Photoshop to map out placement of the sink, countertop, and appliances. The compact kitchen uses every inch of available space and manages to accommodate full-size appliances.

"Custom-made" is a term you hear a lot at Jill's. Because of her patience, selectivity, and desire to maximize her space, nearly every place you look showcases a custom-made solution. A friend made the dining table from an old butcher block and stair banisters. The metal staircase up to the bedroom area came from an architect's office and used to be on wheels. Jill cut it down and painted it to fit in with the decor. She had the bathroom wall rebuilt so it could support a wall-mounted sink.

Jill proves that every obstacle can be overcome and that any space can be turned into a home. Her apartment also shows the importance of enlisting the help of others. This approach is far from the one-stop shopping that Pottery Barn and Home Depot would like you to prefer, and it makes for interior design that reflects an entirely different kind of wealth.

Jill elevated one end of the living area to gain space for storage and to create a stage for performances. The stage surface is painted wheatboard that Jill bought from Bettencourt Wood, *one of the only places in New York that carries green building supplies.* Canal Plastics *fabricated the three doors at the front of the stage. They are attached with* Rare Earth Magnets.

jill's
survey

Style

My style is such that if someone else has it, I usually don't want it.

Inspiration

Places I have lived around the world and people with confidence.

Favorite Element

The steel beam in the middle of my bedroom. When I moved in, my friend and I destroyed the drywall column around the beam with our own hands and feet.

Biggest Challenge

Getting the apartment to a finished state.

What Friends Say

"You are truly insane and talented."

Biggest Embarrassment

It has taken me two years and counting to install a light fixture above the medicine cabinet and to host a housewarming party.

Proudest DIY

My stage . . . It was the first time I used two-by-fours and built something that required a bit of engineering and that, when finished, one could walk on and crawl under.

Biggest Indulgence

My lovely, yummy Dux bed. I spent about two years lying on beds all over town until I finally made the decision that this one was the best. And it is. Every night when I leap into bed, I am reminded of what a good decision it was to buy it.

Best Advice

Get a walk-in closet and put everything inside it.

Dream Source

The back alley when the Prague Municipal Building decides to renovate.

(top left) This area of the apartment, above the bathroom and kitchen, was originally for storage. Jill removed the drywall that encased the I-beam and painted and finished the space to make her bedroom. Next to the old valise are two Chinese opium pillows that Jill bought in Inverness, California. The rug is from Crete, where Jill spent a semester abroad in college.

Jill inherited the 1972 convertible couch (left) from her aunt, who was downsizing her possessions. Jill loves the wide corduroy. The couch is flanked by two Army Corps of Engineers carts that serve as side tables. Arranged on both window-sills are tiles from Mexico, Spain, Israel, England, and the Netherlands.

Jill's media center (above), directly opposite her couch, includes an early-1950s TV that once belonged to her grandfather. The nonfunctioning TV holds her workable CD player and phonograph.

(opposite, top) Jill had the original kitchen completely gutted. She was determined to make the small space feel open but wanted it to contain as much as it did before without using overhead cabinets. A friend built the stainless steel shelving below the counter. Jill used glass from Absolute Glass & Mirrors *for the shelves and for those near the ceiling. The brackets for the upper shelf are from* Sid's Hardware. *Jill keeps beans and rice in salvaged lab bottles from* The Liquidators. *The soapstone countertop is heat-resistant and stain-resistant, and does not need to be sealed. When it starts to dull, she rubs it with vegetable oil. The faucet is from the Highland series by* Cifial.

(opposite, bottom left) The dining table was built by a friend from a used butcher block and salvaged pieces of a stair banister turned upside down. The vase is from Crate & Barrel.

(opposite, bottom right) Jill created the sliding bathroom door by sewing trim onto netting and sandwiching the material between two sheets of half-frosted Plexiglas from Canal Plastics. *The sheets are held with the fasteners used to bind documents. The tracking system and other hardware came from* Design Source by Dave Sanders, Sid's Hardware, *and* Weinstein & Holtzman.

Jill's desk (above) is located at the top of the metal steps leading to the bedroom. She bought a custom sheet of antishatter glass, which has thin wires running through it, and placed it on the metal legs from a Russian sewing-machine table. The ergonomically designed Zody chair by Haworth *is made of recyclable materials. It was important to Jill to find a sustainable product.*

RESOURCES

ABSOLUTE GLASS & MIRRORS: 718.376.8868
BETTENCOURT WOOD: bettencourtwood.com
CANAL PLASTICS: canalplasticscenter.com
CIFIAL: cifialusa.com
CRATE & BARREL: crateandbarrel.com
DESIGN SOURCE BY DAVE SANDERS: davesanders.com
DUX: duxiana.com
HAWORTH: haworth.com
RARE EARTH MAGNETS: rare-earth-magnets.com
SID'S HARDWARE: 718.875.2259
THE LIQUIDATORS: theliquidators.biz
WEINSTEIN & HOLTZMAN: doorsframesandhardware.com

photos by
jonathan lo

21.
jonathan's
'60s retro

floor plan labels:

bedroom
bathroom
closet
bathroom
closet
kitchen
dining area
garage
living area
laundry
bathroom
closet
(second floor)
bedroom
entrance
(first floor)

NAME: **JONATHAN LO**
PROFESSION: **ART DIRECTOR**
LOCATION: **IRVINE, CALIFORNIA**
OWNED/RENTED: **OWNED**
SIZE: **1,200 SQUARE FEET**
TYPE: **NEW 2-BEDROOM TOWNHOUSE**
YEARS LIVED IN: **4**

When Jonathan designed the guest room
(opposite, right), he started with the **IKEA** couch.
For the pillows, he adopted the color scheme from
a midcentury vintage decorating book. Some
pillows are made from **Crate & Barrel** remnant
fabrics; others are from **IKEA** and **Thomas Paul.**
He found the bamboo shades at the local Japanese
supermarket. The lamp, retrieved from the trash,
has a **Martha Stewart for Kmart** shade. The coffee
tables are stacking cubes from **Target.** Jonathan
found the artwork above the couch at a thrift store.

The screen (opposite, far right) looks like metal,
but Jonathan couldn't afford to commission a
metal-smith to create it, so he went the DIY route.
The circles are embroidery hoops hot-glued to wood
dowels. He then painted everything white.

When we first saw Jonathan's house, we were blown away by his use of bright, sunny colors.

His style was infectious, complex, and unlike anything we'd seen before. When we were later seeking a new editor for our LA Web site, Jonathan was the first person we e-mailed to ask for a recommendation. We ended up signing Jonathan on. He now shares his remarkable design sense and optimism with us online at *AT:LA*.

Jonathan chose to express his offbeat design approach in a brand-new suburban home in Orange County. Without making any major interior changes or spending a lot of money, he has used paint, lighting, and furnishings to create a cozy, lived-in feeling.

Jonathan has three secrets for using color: One, if you use only a single color, repeat it in more than one room so it doesn't seem random or jarring. Two, don't be afraid to mix tints, shades, and textures, as this creates complexity. Three, when using a lot of color, allow a space for the eye to rest so you don't overload the room. Jon has kept most of the walls and furniture white or neutral to achieve this effect. As with a number of other homes in this book, a room seems more colorful when surrounded by restful white surfaces.

Jonathan also brings a strong graphic background to decorating his walls. Many interior designers would simply paint an accent wall or hang a picture at a presentable height. Jonathan uses different effects on different parts of a wall. He paints a corner only or extends a color stripe all the way around a room. He paints a small geometric area of a corner to emphasize a shelf and the colorful items on display. In every room, he has created isolated highlights that draw your attention. If you are feeling stuck about bringing color into your rooms, yet are afraid to paint a whole wall, you will find many lessons here.

jonathan's
survey

Style

A modern eclectic mess.

Inspiration

Midcentury idealism mixed with modern comfort. I got a lot of ideas from old DIY decorating books from the '60s and '70s.

Favorite Element

It's very light and bright.

Biggest Challenge

I didn't want to invest too much money into any sort of major customization. The biggest challenge was trying not to make it feel like I'm living in a typical suburban tract home, and still be on a budget.

What Friends Say

"It's so happy in here."

Biggest Embarrassment

Everything is hiding in the closet. I also have way too many pillows and vases.

Proudest DIY

The circle screen made of embroidery hoops and dowels. It's amazing what you can do with a glue gun.

Biggest Indulgence

I spent the most money on my couch.

Best Advice

Go with your gut and take a step back and look at it again.

Dream Source

Any of the modern home design places I read about in British *ELLE Decoration* or in the Japanese design mags.

At the dining room doorway, where the color band ends, Jonathan painted a plant motif on a gray rectangle (bottom, left). The dining room table and chairs are from **IKEA**. *The dresser is a midcentury score from a thrift store. The wall hanging with birds is from an antique store.*

(opposite) The first things Jonathan wants you to look at in his guest room/ retreat are the tall 1980s lamp he found at a thrift store and his admittedly cheesy but comfortable **Pier 1** *papasan chair. Jonathan replaced the bulbs in the lamp with larger globe lights because the original covers were missing. He painted the wall with* **Behr's** *Orange Sovereign to frame the chair and lamp. The shaggy pillow on the floor is from* **Urban Outfitters,** *and the orange one is from* **Crate & Barrel.** *The curtains are from* **Pottery Barn.**

The **IKEA** *shelves (below, top) above the credenza show off some of Jonathan's collection. He has organized the items by color, putting the white vases at the top to keep the arrangement from feeling too heavy. Jonathan found the lamp at an estate sale. He kept the original shade because he liked the ribbon trim that someone glued around the top. The* **Urban Outfitters** *beaded curtain leads to the bathroom. The oatmeal carpeting in the bedrooms and on the stairs was part of the original townhouse construction.*

(below, bottom) In the second-floor living room, Jonathan painted a stripe around the room to which he applied different materials, including cork, mirror, and textured wallpaper. The shag rug is from **IKEA,** *and the couch is from* **Plummers.** *Jonathan made the hanging light by hot-gluing vellum to a wire frame.*

The shelf mounted on the kitchen's half wall (above) is an **IKEA** CD rack. It is Jonathan's approximation of a mantel over a fireplace. He likes the horizontal lines and how they play off the horizontals in the rest of the living room. On top of the rack is a cluster of **CB2** glass candleholders, and inside it is a collection of toys. Jonathan found the 1960s hooked rug at a garage sale. For the area of the living room opposite the couch (right), Jonathan built a low platform table to house his TV and stereo. The midcentury wood room divider caught Jonathan's attention at the Home Consignment Center, where it was displayed amid a sea of mid-1980s Southwest-style couches. Its built-in lamps provide great light in the evening.

The headboard (above) consists of two wooden closet doors from **Home Depot** that Jonathan finished with a cherry gel stain. To make the headboard appear to float, he wedged a piece of wood between the doors and the wall and put a strip of fluorescent lights behind the doors. The bedside tables are from **Crate & Barrel**, and the small lamp is from **IKEA**. Jonathan removed the legs from the credenza because he wanted a low-slung dresser. He created the hanging light by suspending **Pier 1** wind chimes from embroidery hoops painted dark brown. The section of wall in the far corner is painted with Daplin, and American Tradition Signature Colors from **Lowe's**, to activate the shelving.

RESOURCES

BEHR: behr.com

CB2: cb2.com

CRATE & BARREL: crateandbarrel.com

ELLE DECORATION: pointclickhome.com/elle_decor

HOME CONSIGNMENT CENTER: 949.448.8640

HOME DEPOT: homedepot.com

IKEA: ikea.com

KMART: kmart.com

LOWE'S: lowes.com

PIER 1: pier1.com

PLUMMERS: plummers.com

POTTERY BARN: potterybarn.com

TARGET: target.com

THOMAS PAUL: thomaspaul.com

URBAN OUTFITTERS: urbanoutfitters.com

photos by
joseph
desler costa

22.
joseph's wicker nest

office area

living area

(stairs)

dining area

bedroom area

closet

kitchen

bathroom

entrance

NAME: JOSEPH DESLER COSTA
PROFESSION: PHOTOGRAPHER/MUSICIAN
LOCATION: WICKER PARK, CHICAGO
OWNED/RENTED: RENTED
SIZE: 350 SQUARE FEET
TYPE: STUDIO IN A 4-FLAT BROWNSTONE
BUILT IN 1864
YEARS LIVED IN: 1

(opposite) Joseph's favorite piece is the
sofa designed by Peter Hvidt. The wall-
hung shelves from IKEA hold his library.
An Eames side table from eBay sits on a
neutral IKEA rug. The IKEA glass globe
lamp on the floor is the perfect solution for
lighting the edge of the low-ceilinged space.

It's an old saw that painting your walls white will make your space feel larger, but it really does work. Joseph's nest, with its white walls, white floor, and white ceiling, proves the point. The sunlight reflects off the white surfaces and makes his small rooftop apartment seem airy. He doesn't let the color become too uniform, however. Rather than paint the ceiling duct, he left it dark to play up the length of the room.

Joseph's way of arranging the long, narrow space not only is workable but turns the shape into a remarkable design feature. To further open up the space, he eliminated all interior doors, which would have blocked both the view and the light. A sliding drape hides the bedroom area.

The big lesson here is to go with your space's strengths and accentuate what you've got. In Joseph's case, it's the unique length and pitched ceiling with skylights. When you approach your space this way, you can overcome any deficit.

...painting your walls white will make your space feel larger.

Joseph's lounge (above, left) is
a **Sears** knockoff of the famous
Eames design. He found it
at a garage sale. He stores CDs
and DVDs in an **IKEA** kitchen
cabinet mounted in a location on
the wall that would otherwise
be unusable. The niche is a good
spot for electronics. In a small
home, it's a bonus when these
items don't take up floor space.

Joseph painted the walls,
ceiling, and floors (above, right)
with glossy white deck paint
from Home Depot.

(opposite, bottom) The kitchen is located at one end of the long main room. The generous skylight provides natural light in the work area. The wooden counter used for food prep is from **IKEA**. *The tall cabinet with white doors, a wardrobe from* **IKEA**, *serves as a pantry. Since the space has no closets, Joseph lined a wall in the bathroom with several more wardrobes to store the majority of his stuff.*

The dining set (below) is made up of **Eames** *pieces purchased from a friend. The paper ceiling lamp is from* **IKEA**. *Joseph calls the wall-mounted blue object from* **IKEA** *a "vol-key-no" because he uses it to hold his keys when he's at home.*

joseph's
survey

Style

Simple, found items, hand-me-downs, estate sales, rustic clean, Euro simple. I was raised by a packrat grandmother and a mother who threw everything away. So I am a packrat that hides everything so I can't see it or remember where I hid it.

Inspiration

Bright color, white, tree house, igloo.

Favorite Element

My sofa. It's a Peter Hvidt, a Danish modern item.

Biggest Challenge

Creating a private sleeping area in such an open attic-style living space. The sliding curtains allowed me to do this.

What Friends Say

"Space-age bachelor pad."

Biggest Embarrassment

Maybe a little too much IKEA.

Proudest DIY

Although the curtains are crooked, I hung them myself.

Biggest Indulgence

My Sears imitation Eames lounge chair. It's so comfortable.

Best Advice

Find a place for your clutter. If you can't, hide it behind chairs and beds. What I can't see doesn't bother me.

Dream Source

The future . . .

RESOURCES

EBAY: ebay.com

HOME DEPOT: homedepot.com

IKEA: ikea.com

SEARS: sears.com

What I can't
see doesn't
bother me.

(opposite, top) The red chair came from the university that Joseph attended. The small area to the side is just the right size for his computer work space and file storage.

(opposite, bottom left) The bedroom is under the eaves off the main room. The vintage metal bookcase is from a thrift store. The table lamp, part of a pair, is Danish. The other one is in the office area. Behind the door is a small clothes closet.

Creating a private sleeping area (bottom) was Joseph's biggest challenge. His solution was to use window treatments as a room divider (left). He bought the panels and the track at **IKEA**. *The apartment's second skylight is above the bed. Even when the panels are closed, they allow filtered light into the main space. The bed and linens are from* **IKEA**.

photos by
jill slater

23.
justine and david's home away from home

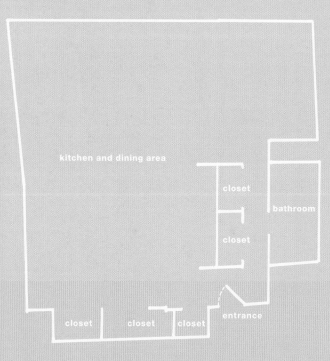

kitchen and dining area

closet

bathroom

closet

closet   closet   closet   entrance

NAME: JUSTINE AND DAVID
PROFESSION: HUMAN RESOURCES MANAGER (JUSTINE) AND SOFTWARE DESIGNER (DAVID)
LOCATION: FINANCIAL DISTRICT, MANHATTAN, NYC
OWNED/RENTED: RENTED
SIZE: 1,200 SQUARE FEET
TYPE: LOFT IN A 6-STORY 1990s BUILDING
YEARS LIVED IN: 2

(opposite) The Mongolian boots are from the Alameda Flea Market. The shelves are accessible both from inside the kitchen and from Justine's painting corner.

Justine and David are nesters with style. They are also at once nomadic, extremely picky, and unsentimental about stuff. Now that they've created a remarkable home in downtown New York, they are ready to move on.

Justine and David met while living in San Francisco. After they got married, they moved to New York, into their first shared apartment. David is British, and Justine is French, and between the two of them, they have been away from their respective homelands for fourteen years. Even though they're unsentimental about possessions, they love what they end up keeping. David, a former architect, has an apartment's worth of high modern furniture packed in storage in London.

Justine, who has moved nine times over the past eight years, is very practical and somewhat wary of acquiring anything she has to move again. That said, she has a penchant for antique wrenches.

Their home isn't their ideal rental. Both prefer a space with more character. But in New York, you pay extra for character, so, in a rush to find housing, they settled for a new purpose-built loft space in Lower Manhattan. The day they moved in, they unpacked completely, and the place hasn't changed a bit since.

The loft's white boxiness goes almost unnoticed. Instead, Justine and David's

carefully considered belongings attract all the attention. When we first saw this apartment, we were struck by the white and yellow space-age dining chairs. As we spent more time in the loft, we found more and more pieces of interest. It is their funky collection, not the attributes of the physical space, that defines their home.

Justine and David will tell you that "it is more fun to be nomadic," and we can see why. There is a freshness to this home that stems from its impermanence. We're just glad they stayed long enough for us to visit!

*Situated near the apartment's entrance are a dining table and chairs from the **Alameda Flea Market**. The only repair necessary was spraying the legs with silver paint.*

justine and david's
survey

Style

We like wood and rusted objects mixed with modern things. We always feel at home because we have a collection of David's drawings, paintings from Justine's family members, and a wall of family pictures.

Inspiration

Wherever we find ourselves. Things miraculously assembled together when we moved in, and the white space allowed lots of freedom.

Favorite Elements

Two large cats, our air mattress for guests, Justine's wrench collection, and David's record collection.

Biggest Challenge

Living together as a couple sometimes brings challenges. We have different tastes and have opposite sleeping patterns. One of our challenges is the absence of a bedroom separated by walls.

What Friends Say

"Can I come to NY and sleep at your house?"

Biggest Embarrassment

It feels like we are in a big yuppie loft. Also, we haven't made the best use of it. Justine wishes she had more time to paint, for example, and David wishes he spent more time listening to his records.

Proudest DIY

Aerial view of Manhattan on the floor made by David. A wooden table with two wheels—Justine got it for five dollars because it was soaking wet. She dried it, sanded it, and renailed it. Now we love it!

Biggest Indulgence

The rent!

Best Advice

Share your house! Next time you go on vacation, do an apartment swap. David and I had a great holiday in Paris living in someone's apartment, while this person was in our apartment. It gives new perspective to live in someone else's space. For doing apartment swaps, www.itamos.com is a great Web site.

Dream Sources

Flea markets and garage sales; seeing old objects in a flea market tells us a lot about the history of America.

David and Justine, recent New York transplants, are fascinated by every nook and cranny in the city. David purchased two copies of a book of satellite photos of Manhattan and re-created the entire borough on the floor of the living area (below, left). Acetate, taped down at the edges, protects the photos and holds them in place. The white **Bertoia** chairs are from a thrift store and a midcentury modern store in San Francisco. David's desk is from the **Alameda Flea Market**.

David's DJ corner (below, right) is an **IKEA** shelving unit on wheels. He and Justine put other pieces of furniture on wheels to facilitate spontaneous rearranging.

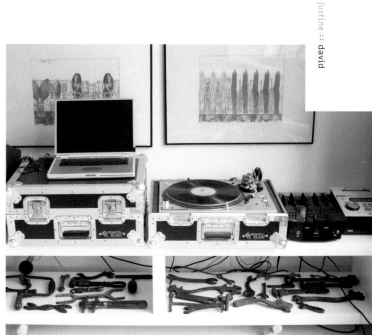

The chest (left) used as a coffee table is from a thrift store in San Francisco. David and Justine attached it to a wooden box they bought on **eBay** and then put it on wheels. The red chair is from the **Alameda Flea Market**.

Justine likes to collect wrenches and has hundreds of them. Fortunately, her employer paid for her move from San Francisco to New York. The movers insisted on protecting each wrench individually in bubble wrap, despite Justine's insistence that the tools would be fine if thrown about en route.

As renters, Justine and David quietly tolerate their all-black kitchen.

Justine in the living area, on a couch from **Room & Board**. *The loft has a great balcony that runs along the entire length. Although the apartment is in the Financial District and surrounded by tall buildings, it gets a tremendous amount of natural light.*

Another fortuitous flea market find holds small treasures.

Justine's painting area (left) faces the bedroom. The IKEA *bamboo wall and a bamboo rug from* Crate & Barrel *serve as makeshift walls to create privacy. The chair and table are from the* Alameda Flea Market.

The rake (below) was a gift from Justine's friend Cori, who collects garden tools. The saw is from the Alameda Flea Market, *and the paddle is from a San Francisco garage sale.*

...objects in a flea market tell us a lot about the history of America.

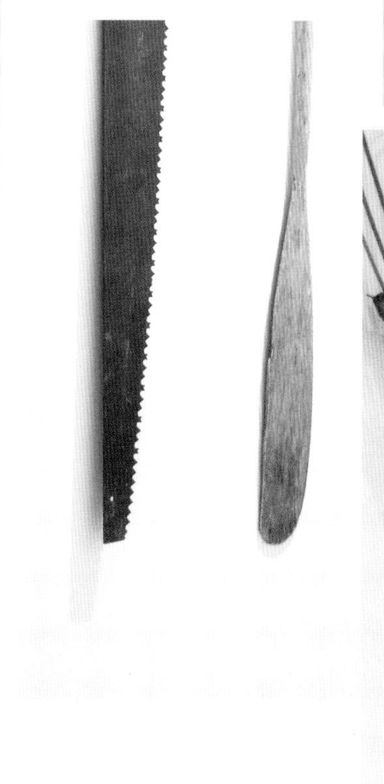

RESOURCES

ALAMEDA FLEA MARKET: antiquesbybay.com
CRATE & BARREL: crateandbarrel.com
EBAY: ebay.com
IKEA: ikea.com
ROOM & BOARD: roomandboard.com

photos by
marilyn
and peter frank

24.
marilyn and peter's home studio

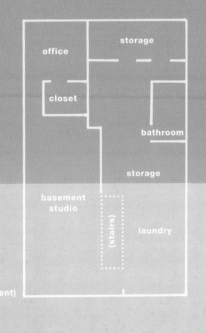

closet

bedroom

bedroom

closet

art studio

bathroom

kitchen

(stairs)

living room

dining room

(1st floor)

entrance

office

storage

closet

bathroom

storage

basement studio

(stairs)

laundry

(basement)

NAME: MARILYN AND PETER FRANK
PROFESSION: ARTISTS AND OWNERS
OF F2 ART & DESIGN
LOCATION: SKOKIE, ILLINOIS
OWNED/RENTED: OWNED
SIZE: 2,200 SQUARE FEET
TYPE: 2-BEDROOM RANCH-STYLE HOME
BUILT IN 1951
YEARS LIVED IN: 6

(opposite, left) Marilyn and Peter dedicate one room to their art studio/work space. Here and throughout the home, they like glass surfaces for easy cleanup. All the tables and the globe lights are from CB2. *The trash bins are from* Design Within Reach, *and the round storage unit is a reissue of a 1971 piece by* Kartell.

There is something ethereal about Marilyn and Peter's home. The rooms are light and airy, the furniture is soft and rounded, and every room is extremely balanced and well organized. You feel as if you could move in for a rest cure.

Marilyn and Peter are artists who fled the big city (NYC), looking for more space. They found it in Skokie, where they have created their dream home studio inside a vintage ranch house that offers them the room they never had. Their current aesthetic aligns perfectly with their suburban home: the '50s are back in style. Part of the surprise of Marilyn and Peter's successful design is their use of white as a color. Bright color occurs incidentally, in furnishings and accessories, and the white walls softly surround each space.

Although they have much more space than they did in New York, Marilyn and Peter have struggled to avoid stuffing each room. Being artists who design and produce glass artwork, they will tell you that they have made and collected so many things that they have an overflowing storage area. Their living spaces, however, are carefully considered, and each is clearly defined. Everything has a place. For example, their CD and book collections are large, but are so well organized in attractive shelving that they add to the look of the room.

You may be surprised about Marilyn and Peter's resources. The stylishness of their home suggests that they purchased furniture from high-end shops, but the source they used most often is IKEA. With careful selection and application of furnishings – so that an individual piece doesn't stand out – the Swedish Giant can be an amazing provider of building blocks we all can use in our homes.

A painting by Peter (below) hangs in the art studio. The glass-topped worktables hold both decorative and utilitarian items. Marilyn and Peter used Ultra White by Behr on the walls throughout the house for its light-reflecting properties.

Marilyn and Peter think of their basement as a self-contained studio apartment. The Case Studies daybed is from Modernica, *and the* Pier Design *coffee table is from* Design Within Reach. *The pale green and dark green* Armstrong *tiles were placed randomly on the floor to create a "punch card" effect.* IKEA *shelving units hold CDs and vintage TVs. The acrylic swivel chair is from* Las Venus. *The stools are from* Totem. *The white* Vitra Utensilo *organizer was found on* eBay, *and the* Nelson *clock is from* Design Within Reach.

(opposite, top) Marilyn and Peter host dinner parties at the glass-topped table in the basement. The orange chairs are from an office furniture store in Jersey City. They bought the round white chair at Weekend Records *in Wicker Park. The wall of bookshelves is made up of two* IKEA *shelving units.*

(opposite, bottom left) Next to the basement couch is a blown-glass lamp that Marilyn and Peter designed and their company, F2 Art & Design, *produces. The four Japanese salt and pepper shakers on the side table were purchased over different visits to the* Broadway Antique Market *in Chicago. The bamboo screen is from* IKEA.

marilyn and peter's
survey

Inspiration

Keeping the vibe of the era in which our house was built, while integrating timeless pieces with current, minimal, clean aesthetics. It is a place for us to produce, display, and house our creative projects.

Favorite Elements

The sitting area in the basement (*Marilyn*) and the art studio (*Peter*).

Biggest Challenge

Our home was built in the 1950s, so it's designed in typical "small" fashion for the period: small entryways, small hallways, small doorways, small closets, small rooms. If we're not careful, we can easily crowd our spaces with too much furniture and too many possessions; therefore, everything we own is thoroughly considered for size, placement, aesthetics, and overall effect.

What Friends Say

"When can we come over?"

Biggest Embarrassment

We have too many things in storage that we should deal with. Mostly it's a time issue.

Proudest DIY

The basement renovation.

Biggest Indulgence

Space. Having lived in NYC for a number of years, we always wished we had more space. Now that we do, we are grateful . . . although it's allowed us to collect far more than we intended!

Best Advice

Both given and received — white IS a color!

Dream Sources

Luminaire, Poliform, Orange Skin, Scout, Moss, BDDW, and Gansevoort Gallery, and in Miami, Galerie Emmanuel Perrotin.

Peter found the piece of marble (left) on the side of the road. He smoothed it with a belt sander and then set it on top of an aluminum planter from Chiasso. *The chair is a discontinued design by* Quinze and Milan, *from* Orange Skin. *Peter made the painting above the chair.*

After spending many years
in a loft, Marilyn and Peter
feel comfortable creating
multipurpose rooms like
this dining/living room on
the main floor (right). The
credenza is from IKEA. The
couch is by Periphere in
Canada.

The IKEA bed (below) from
the Malm series is oak
veneer. The walnut veneer
bedside tables are from a
now-closed Chicago store.
They hold glass lamps made
by Marilyn and Peter and
wood box clocks by Furnie
from Hejfina. The George
Nelson bench is from Design
Within Reach. The large
wood acupuncture model
came from an acupuncturist's
window display in
Manhattan's Chinatown.

The lamps (left) were in Marilyn's parents' house for thirty-five years and are considered family heirlooms. Rather than replace the tattered lampshades, Marilyn and Peter decided to put in clear globes and leave them naked for a "futuristic look."

Below is one of two informal dining areas in the house. Marilyn and Peter put a glass top over an IKEA melamine table. The two Eames chairs are from Modernica. The other two chairs, by Werner Panton and Ron Arad, were purchased at a Chicago Museum of Contemporary Arts employee-only sample sale. The two IKEA glass cabinets are full of curiosities such as vintage beakers, coral, crystal, a Lladro elephant, a Jonathan Adler vase, and some glass pieces by Marilyn and Peter.

RESOURCES

ARMSTRONG: armstrong.com

BDDW: bddw.com

BEHR: behr.com

BROADWAY ANTIQUE MARKET: bamchicago.com

CB2: cb2.com

CHIASSO: chiasso.com

DESIGN WITHIN REACH: dwr.com

EBAY: ebay.com

F2 ART & DESIGN: f2.cc

GALERIE EMMANUEL PERROTIN: galerieperrotin.com

HEJFINA: hejfina.com

IKEA: ikea.com

JONATHAN ADLER: jonathanadler.com

KARTELL: kartell.it

LAS VENUS: lasvenus.com

LLADRO: lladro.com

LUMINAIRE: luminaire.com

MODERNICA: modernica.net

MOSS: mossonline.com

ORANGE SKIN: orangeskin.com

PERIPHERE: periphere.com

POLIFORM: poliformusa.com

SCOUT: scoutchicago.com

TOTEM: totemdesign.com

VITRA: vitra.com

photos by
jill slater

25.
marlon's
blue pad

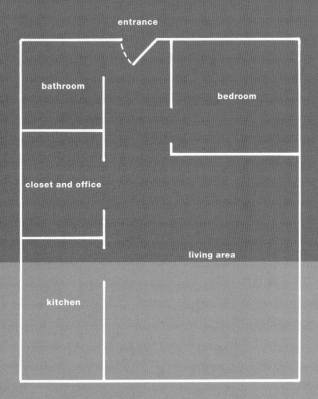

entrance

bathroom

bedroom

closet and office

living area

kitchen

NAME: MARLON
PROFESSION: COMPANY DIRECTOR
AT THOM BROWNE
LOCATION: CHELSEA, NYC
OWNED/RENTED: RENTED
SIZE: 650 SQUARE FEET
TYPE: 1-BEDROOM IN A LARGE PREWAR
APARTMENT BUILDING
YEARS LIVED IN: 3

Marlon's intense and unusual style
may not be for everyone,
but you *have* to appreciate his total vision
and consistency.

He shows us – through the responses his apartment provokes – how powerful interior design can be.

The power of Marlon's pad comes from high contrasts, surprising art, and the Hermes blue on the walls. Strong colors like this are hard to decorate with, but this one is more subtle than a cloying primary hue and has a vintage feel. Marlon uses the blue in nearly every room as the main element that pulls everything together.

The dark walls are set off with white trim and ceilings, as well as white furniture, a contrast that heightens the vibrancy of the deep color. If you want to make a room come to life with paint alone, pushing the contrast between the walls and the trim and ceiling, as Marlon has done, will have a guaranteed effect.

Then there is the art. Art and design are Marlon's passion. He has surrounded himself with icons from both the commercial and the spiritual worlds – a combination meant to provoke as much as inspire, but, again, his choices are impeccable. Andy Warhol would have liked having drinks here.

More than anything else, we love Marlon's choice of old-fashioned chandeliers, which he made himself. Everything else in his home is modern and masculine, and the chandeliers offer an elegant and feminine counterpoint that sweetens the space.

marlon's
survey

Style

To surround myself with things that are beautifully made and personally inspiring.

Inspiration

Contemporary art.

Favorite Element

The art in the apartment.

Biggest Challenge

I have to edit my ideas and choices down because there aren't more rooms to decorate.

What Friends Say

They say that it's very Marlon.

Biggest Embarrassment

The shirts in the refrigerator.

Proudest DIY

The chandeliers.

Biggest Indulgence

The plasma screen TV, but it's hard to say because it's all decadent.

Best Advice

Dimmers make every room look better.

Dream Source

The Guggenheim's basement.

Marlon's living room is filled with late-1960s furniture, including the couch, two chairs, and the coffee table, which once belonged to a couple in Seattle. Marlon bought the whole set right out of their backyard, sun stains and all. He had the couch and chairs reupholstered in black leather and painted white. The wall color is a custom mix that approximates Hermes blue. Marlon made the sconces as well as all the chandeliers. He started with a basic Lucite chandelier from one of the many Bowery lighting stores, then added all sorts of baubles and beads. For the finishing touch, he used small brown shades.

andy warhol would have liked having drinks here.

In the living room (above, left), Marlon paired two photographs by **Jill Greenberg**. The standing white speakers are **Minipods**. The matching glass skulls on the coffee table are vintage bookends.

Marlon had his eye on these **Conran** chairs (above, right) years ago when he saw them in the basement of the Seattle Science Center while working on a freelance project. The center gave them to Marlon as a token of appreciation. The chairs are a perfect match for his living room set. The pillows were inspired by expensive *Gucci* versions. Marlon found a huge old fur coat at a church thrift sale and brought it to a tailor, who was so amused by the project that she went out of her way to do a great job. The **Saarinen** table displays a **Williams-Sonoma** bowl laden with garage-sale ceramic fruit.

There is no greater proof that the apartment is occupied by a New York City bachelor than this appliance (right). Marlon never eats at home, so he quickly came to see his kitchen as untapped storage. He keeps all his shirts in the refrigerator (they are all crisp and cool for the sake of the ice cream in the freezer), his towels in one cabinet, and his sheets in another.

The bedroom is small, about eight feet square. Marlon bought the matching mirrors (above) from **Housing Works**, painted them, and then added wooden guns made by a Brooklyn-based artist. His bed consists of four bolsters from **Design Within Reach**.

(right) This is one of the sconces in the living room. Marlon's proud of how over-the-top they are. The biggest challenge, he said, was figuring out where to stop.

The deer in the bedroom (below) is from the **Hell's Kitchen Flea Market**. *These walls, a deeper color than those in the main room, are painted in* **Janovic's** *Shark Skin.*

Marlon put this piece together (below, middle) after seeing work by **Toland Grinnell,** *an artist known for elaborately transformed traveling trunks. This trunk belonged to Marlon's grandmother. His turntables fit perfectly on top. He bought a cheap* **Louis Vuitton** *knockoff bag in Chinatown and cut record-sized discs to place on each turntable.*

RESOURCES

CONRAN: conran.com

DESIGN WITHIN REACH: dwr.com

HELL'S KITCHEN FLEA MARKET: hellskitchenfleamarket.com

HOUSING WORKS: housingworks.org

JANOVIC: janovic.com

JILL GREENBERG: manipulator.com

MINIPODS: minipods.com

WILLIAMS-SONOMA: williams-sonoma.com

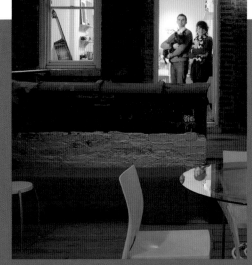

photos by
evan thomas

26.
melissa and matt's design lab

NAME: MELISSA SHOCKLEY
AND MATT RIDDLE
PROFESSION: DESIGNER AND MODERN
FURNITURE SALES (MELISSA) AND
GRAPHIC DESIGNER (MATT)
LOCATION: RIVER WEST, CHICAGO
OWNED/RENTED: RENTED
SIZE: 550 SQUARE FEET
TYPE: 1-BEDROOM IN A LATE
20TH-CENTURY BUILDING
YEARS LIVED IN: 1

Full disclosure — it was Melissa and Matt's bedroom that drew us in. The contrast of blue and yellow, based on a dress of Melissa's, was a total surprise. Once we left the bedroom, we could see that other rooms have similar small and large contrasts that add edge and interest. Among these little visual experiments are novel applications of wall graphics, a hot red medicine cabinet, and a professional espresso station.

In all other ways, however, this apartment is spartan and a good example of simple living. Melissa and Matt have worked hard to organize their storage and reduce clutter. The things that they do have, they are eager to put on display. Many objects are shown off in vignettes, and each comes with a story or gains a story because of what is next to it. For example, a funky bean bag chair sits on a small patch of carpet with a lamp and a bookcase. A wall graphic completes this small island, a favorite place to sit and relax. This kind of relationship building between objects creates harmony.

melissa and matt's
survey

Style

Our style is really based on what the space will allow. Some things that never change are the sentimental objects that remind us of friends and family, our travels, and good times. Trying to make those things fit into the space we're living in usually dictates the overall aesthetic.

Inspiration

A piece of artwork that was given to Melissa by a dear friend. It's the perfect combination of shapes and colors.

Favorite Element

Melissa's string bass.

Biggest Challenge

Far and away, the limitations of the furniture arrangement. The main space is about three times as long as it is wide. We've tried to do a lot of things to keep it from feeling like a bowling alley and to give the eye several places to land before hitting the end of the room.

What Friends Say

We get a lot of comments about the lack of clutter.

Biggest Embarrassment

By far, our sad, sad bathroom. There's no space, no storage, and it's just a nightmare. We mostly keep that door closed.

Proudest DIY

Melissa made all the pillows in the space.

Biggest Indulgence

Most recently, the Eames Sofa Compact. We acquired it under very "cosmic" circumstances. Melissa told someone we wanted one and they said, "Oh, I have a friend that's selling one." Sight unseen, it was delivered in beautiful condition and in a very livable upholstery.

Best Advice

Stick with what you really love. If you start with a feeling or an object that you like, and just keep it simple, it will all come together.

Dream Source

For "stuff" it's a toss-up between Unica Home and Rotofugi.

The Eames Sofa Compact (above) anchors the main living area. Melissa and Matt bought the two green end tables years ago from Urban Outfitters for twenty dollars. Melissa had to have the small yarn-wrapped stool from IKEA. The counter is decorated with blik wall decals, which Melissa cut to create the pattern across the bar.

The bookshelf (opposite, inset) is made from the modular Cubits line from Design Within Reach. The various storage containers are from IKEA and the Container Store. Melissa picked up the striking red branch at Jayson Home & Garden a few years ago. It has always had pride of place in her apartments. Here, it is the perfect color counterpoint to the blue wall, painted Winwood Spring by Behr.

Matt won the La Marzocco *espresso machine (above) in the U.S. Barista Championship. It is top-of-the-line and a wonderful appliance to have at home, according to Melissa. It sits on a stainless steel cart from* Design Within Reach. *The painting by* Karen Combs *of* Nama Rococo *is a prized possession.*

The white stools (left) are Last Minute *from* Design Within Reach. *The open shelving was in place when Melissa and Matt moved in. The upper shelf holds one of Matt's photos. In this one Melissa is the subject.*

The Tom Rock rocker (top left) by Ron Arad is from Design Within Reach, as is the Eames coatrack. Melissa has played bass since she was ten.

The bedroom (top right) features a DIY bed and headboard. Melissa painted a simple raw pine bed from IKEA. To make the headboard, she cut four MDF panels, covered them with foam, batting, and yellow velvet, and attached them to the white headboard. Striped curtains cover a closet on one side of the bedroom and a window on the other. The dress form is from Jo-Ann Fabrics. Above the bed hangs a silkscreen by Amos Kennedy, Jr.

The bright red medicine cabinet (above, left) from IKEA has a cutout section that Melissa uses for a jewelry display. A photo by Matt hangs above a clock from Unica Home. The makeup/shaving mirror is from IKEA, as is the red "octopus" hanger suspended from the shower curtain bar.

A Magiker cabinet (above, right) from IKEA holds electronics. The office has a clever workstation assembled from Elfa pieces from the Container Store. The Caper task chair is from Herman Miller.

Melissa used a blik *decal as a stencil to create a clever play on positive and negative space. She affixed the decal to the wall, painted the dark stripe over it, carefully cut the decal along the edge of the stripe, and removed the right portion of the decal under the dark paint. The stripe color is Pewter Mug by* Behr. *The rug was created with* Flor *modular carpet tiles. The* FatBoy *bean bag chair makes this a favorite spot to relax in the office. A module from the* Design Within Reach *Cubits line serves as a side table.*

melissa :: matt

RESOURCES

BEHR: behr.com

BLIK: whatisblik.com

CONTAINER STORE: containerstore.com

DESIGN WITHIN REACH: dwr.com

FATBOY: fatboy.nl

FLOR: florcatalog.com

HERMAN MILLER: hermanmiller.com

IKEA: ikea.com

JAYSON HOME & GARDEN: jayson-homegarden.com

JO-ANN FABRICS: joann.com

LA MARZOCCO: lamarzocco.com

NAMA ROCOCO: namarococo.com

ROTOFUGI: rotofugi.com

UNICA HOME: unicahome.com

URBAN OUTFITTERS: urbanoutfitters.com

photos by
amanda wachob

27.
michael and
corrie's
mini mansion

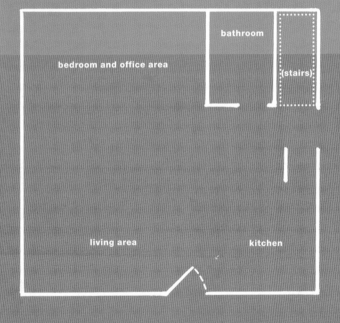

bathroom

bedroom and office area

(stairs)

living area

kitchen

NAME: MICHAEL ZEBROWSKI
AND CORRIE WACHOB
PROFESSION: PROFESSOR OF
ARCHITECTURE AND WOODWORKER
(MICHAEL) AND WRITER (CORRIE)
LOCATION: BUFFALO, NEW YORK
OWNED/RENTED: OWNED
SIZE: 440 SQUARE FEET
TYPE: 1951 WOOD-FRAME COTTAGE
WITH A PITCHED ROOF
YEARS LIVED IN: 3

the lesson here is not in objects,
but in how much you can change the space
to make a much bigger home.

Michael and Corrie's home, way up north in the coldest part of New York State, offers a refreshing view of the possibilities that await you when you're ready to tear down the walls and ceiling and build exactly what you want. The tight space forced them to look in unexpected places for more room. Gutting the attic allowed them to raise the ceiling, enlarge the space, and move the storage overhead. It's a design that works beautifully.

We were instantly drawn to their intelligent solutions and especially to the ingenious rolling ladder that leads up to the storage area. Downstairs, we loved how the room is woody and open with dark stained floors and bright, indirect lighting. A lot of new construction can be soulless, but Michael's cabinetry and woodwork give each area a warm handmade feeling.

Given how much work Michael did himself, you won't find many traditional sources here. All the fittings are custom, so the takeaway is all in the ideas and the inspiration. In contrast to the many "collectors" in this book who have cobbled together exquisite collections over time, the lesson here is not in objects, but in how much you can change the space itself to make a much bigger home.

The countertop that holds the sink, like the island countertop, is poured concrete. Underneath it, Michael built inset doors.

Michael added a gate to shield access to the front door. On it he placed this simple, elegant sign with the street number. It is a wood stencil lit from behind.

michael and corrie's
survey

Style

Luckily, living in such a small space, we have a similar aesthetic. We like clean lines, natural materials, and utilitarian designs. We try to stay away from extraneous decorative "things," because our home doesn't allow for too much clutter.

Inspiration

Upon moving back to Buffalo, we discovered that the wooded acres and surrounding farms were being torn down for cheaply built, poorly designed überhomes, while the aging, well-constructed, and inexpensive urban housing stock was being abandoned. We wanted to show that a house doesn't need to be brand-new or monstrously large to be magnificent, and that you don't have to be wealthy to live in a well-designed home.

Favorite Elements

Since we lived in the house while it was under construction, our favorite elements are the ones that we were forced to live without for the longest (like the bathroom door and the kitchen sink), as well as the ones that involve the greatest craftsmanship and exhibit the most flair (like the floors and lighting in the kitchen).

Biggest Challenge

Keeping it simple, functional, and still livable.

What Friends Say

When people come over for the first time and their eyes rise toward the bookshelves and storage spaces, they always say, "Whoa!"

Biggest Embarrassment

The time that it took to finish it all. Entire neighborhoods have been built in the time it took us to finish renovations.

Proudest DIY

After looking into how much store-bought cabinets and countertops would cost, Mike decided to construct his own. Now, he is sole proprietor of Bruce Street Fabrication, specializing in custom residential renovation, particularly cabinets and concrete countertops.

Biggest Indulgence

Doing the renovation. When we bought the house, there was very little money between us, and yet here we were buying beautiful sheets of birch and large quantities of steel. Every material we selected and detail that we added was an indulgence.

Best Advice

During Mike's freshman year as an undergraduate architecture student, he attended a lecture by Edgar Tafel, architect and Frank Lloyd Wright apprentice. He said the best thing to do as a young architect right out of school is to go build your own house.

Dream Source

If you twisted our arms, we'd say any current, modern design company mixed in with retro originals.

The island — a poured concrete slab supported by aluminum legs — helps delineate the kitchen area in the open floor plan. The doors of the cabinets under the island can be opened by foot, keeping the hands free. It is one of the many clever and practical ideas Michael built into the kitchen.

(opposite, top) Michael used the kitchen as a future portfolio, experimenting with different types of cabinets and drawer styles. Hamilton Bay pendants from Home Depot light the kitchen.

Michael built the bed frame (right), side table, dresser, and desk. The bedroom floor is a mix of cherry and black-stained hickory. Michael found the floorboards at an auction. There was just enough wood to make this pattern.

Originally the cottage had eight-foot ceilings and a walk-in attic. Michael, a skilled carpenter and architect, gutted the home, removed the interior walls, and eliminated the attic to create a cathedral ceiling (left). The elevated storage space that he designed and built (above) runs the length of the home and is accessed by a ladder.

181

michael :: corrie

The ladder (left) is an essential component of the storage system. It rolls on a track along the length of the house and provides access to the stereo, books, clothing, and seldom-used kitchen appliances. Michael made the ladder from two pieces of steel angle iron that he cut, bent, and welded. Each steel step has a cap of cherrywood.

The trim for the storage area (above), welded on-site, consists of one-eighth-inch steel sealed with butcher's wax. The wood is Baltic birch plywood. Michael built this part of the house during the first year of construction. The halogen lights that illuminate the books are Hamilton Bay from Home Depot. The other two lights are framed in triangles of birch plywood.

photos by
lane johnson

28.
patrick's
cosmo-urban
studio rental

entrance

bedroom

closet

closet

kitchen

bedroom

living and dining area

NAME: PATRICK J. HAMILTON
PROFESSION: CREATIVE DIRECTOR,
INTERIOR DESIGNER, AND COPYWRITER
LOCATION: UPPER WEST SIDE, NYC
OWNED/RENTED: RENTED
SIZE: 485 SQUARE FEET
TYPE: STUDIO IN A 1985 BUILDING
YEARS LIVED IN: 7

(opposite, left) The bathroom is no less meticulously curated than any other part of Patrick's apartment. The black and white tiles came with the apartment, and rather than fight them, Patrick played off them in his choice of shower curtain and bath mat from Bloomingdale's.

He had the steel table custom made to fit over the toilet.

(opposite, right) The photo by Christopher Makos hangs at the end of the hallway above a Philippe Starck Hudson chair.

Patrick lives and breathes Apartment Therapy. When we first met him, he was digging his small studio out from under many years' accumulation of beautiful things – collecting is a serious hobby. He hired us to consult with him, and then he went to work.

What is remarkable is that the apartment is still quite full, but now is cozy instead of cluttered. Patrick's approach to arranging everything both maximizes the space and conveys a sense of calm. One of his strategies was to create distinct zones. Most studio apartments look like one big room. In Patrick's studio, you have a strong feeling of hallway, living room, and bedroom. Each zone uses accent paint or furniture to separate it from the next.

The ability of colors to contract and expand a space is a great interior design trick.

Instead of placing the sectional against the wall, for instance, he pulled it away from the wall and used it to divide the main space, creating a living room and a small, flexible bar/dining area. Two consoles behind the sofa can be moved and placed together to form a small rectangular dining table.

Patrick's apartment is also a great study in the effectiveness of the color brown. A good brown paint is hard to find, but Patrick picked the right one for use in the entry, hallway, and sleeping alcove. The brown adds warmth and strong focal points. As you sit in the living room, the brown at the end of the hallway to the bathroom attracts your gaze and creates

a pleasing visual moment impossible with white walls.

The dark brown walls also help make the studio appear larger by contracting space. When you are in the hallway, the brown walls seem to come toward you. Then, as you enter the living room, with its white walls, the space opens up. The ability of colors to contract and expand a space is a great interior design trick – and one that is easy to try with just some paint and a brush.

(above) A carefully selected and arranged vignette greets you when you walk into Patrick's apartment. The entry wall is painted in Pratt and Lambert's Loam. Leaning on the macassar ebony console table from Bloomingdale's is a framed William Klein photo that Patrick bought on eyestorm.com. Beneath the console is a storage ottoman by Mitchell Gold from ABC Carpet & Home. The aluminum propeller is from the Golden Nugget Flea Market. Patrick found a man on eBay who mounted the propeller on a base.

Patrick's reading area (right), which enjoys natural light and city views, includes a leather chair and ottoman, and a houndstooth throw from Crate & Barrel. The magazine rack is from Ligne Roset. The round side table, made of plywood, is covered in a burlap blanket that movers left behind after Patrick relocated to the apartment. The lamp is from Conran, and the black shade is from Trans-Lux. Leaning on the wall is a James Welling photograph from eyestorm.com.

The two glass tables (left) behind the couch and the patchwork wooden cabinet in one corner are from **Crate & Barrel.** *The zebra chairs are from a thrift store. Patrick had them reupholstered in a* **Scalamandre** *fabric. The jute rug is from* **Pottery Barn.** *The window treatments consist of solar shades from* **Janovic** *and velvet drapes from* **Hud-son Dry Goods.**

The couch is from **Bloomingdale's** *and the pillows are from* **Pottery Barn.** *The entryway is at the far left.*

patrick's
survey

Style

Collected urban comfort.

Inspiration

Various . . . the machine-age efficiency of Raymond Loewy's train compartments, the regal Egyptian and Nubian tribal contrasts of *Aïda*, the city outside my windows.

Favorite Elements

Bed area, colored accent walls, art, and lighting.

Biggest Challenge

Keeping edited.

What Friends Say

"Very cozy." "Chic and masculine." "Only 485 square feet? Really?!?"

Biggest Embarrassment

My magazine "habit."

Proudest DIY

More like DIWH—Did It With Help. The bed hangings on hospital track defining the bed area and painted accent walls.

Biggest Indulgence

Art collection (contemporary photography) and one Ralph Lauren table . . . bought post-9/11 as a personal contribution to the NYC economy.

Best Advice

Limit your palette, expand your textures. Make every choice an exercise in "compare and contrast."

Dream Sources

VW Home, Terrence Conran Shop, Repertoire, Donghia, William Sofield. Any of the winter art fairs.

Patrick created a U-shaped bedroom alcove using curtains that run on hospital track. The curtains, as well as the headboard, are from **Pottery Barn**. The hospital track is from **Curtain Fair**. All of the bedding comes from **Garnet Hill**.

(opposite) Two totem stools and a glass console form the flexible dining area. An ottoman from **Portico** with a **Pottery Barn** tray functions as a side table and can also be used as extra seating. A second ottoman is tucked below the console. Patrick saw the transit sign in **Banana Republic** and tracked it down at **Blackman Cruz**. The white mirrored cabinet next to the kitchen is from **IKEA**.

The **Ralph Lauren** bedside table (right) is from **Bloomingdale's**. The **Tizio** swiveling lamp is from **Artemide**. Patrick found the head at the **Metropolitan Museum** store. He wanted to add a color accent to the arrangement. A friend found the coral on **eBay** and gave it to Patrick as a gift. The striped stool is from **Repertoire**.

RESOURCES

ABC CARPET & HOME: abchome.com

ARTEMIDE: artemide.com

BLACKMAN CRUZ: blackmancruz.com

BLOOMINGDALE'S: bloomingales.com

CHRISTOPHER MAKOS: makostudio.com

CONRAN: conran.com

CRATE & BARREL: crateandbarrel.com

CURTAIN FAIR: curtainfair.com

DONGHIA: donghia.com

EBAY: ebay.com

EYESTORM: eyestorm.com

GARNET HILL: garnethill.com

GOLDEN NUGGET FLEA MARKET:
gnfleamarket.com

HUDSON DRY GOODS: 212.579.7397

IKEA: ikea.com

JANOVIC: janovic.com

LIGNE ROSET: ligne-roset-usa.com

METROPOLITAN MUSEUM STORE:
metmuseum.org

PHILIPPE STARCK: philippe-starck.com

PORTICO: porticostore.com

POTTERY BARN: potterybarn.com

PRATT AND LAMBERT:
prattandlambert.com

RALPH LAUREN: rlhome.polo.com

REPERTOIRE: 212.941.9101

SCALAMANDRE: scalamandre.com

TRANS-LUX: 212.925.5863

VW HOME FURNITURE: 212.244.5008

photos by
lane johnson

29.
paul's pivoting perfection

living area

entrance · kitchen

dining area

bedroom area

closet

bathroom · office

NAME: PAUL MICHAEL FITZPATRICK, JR.
PROFESSION: PROPERTY MANAGER
FOR INDUSTRIAL, CORPORATE,
AND RETAIL SPACES
LOCATION: WEST VILLAGE, NYC
OWNED/RENTED: OWNED
SIZE: 275 SQUARE FEET
TYPE: STUDIO IN A 5-FLOOR
WALK-UP, BUILT IN 1879
YEARS LIVED IN: 3

Paul's tiny, narrow, ground-floor apartment displays the finest use of a Murphy bed and the tightest design we've seen to date. Benefiting from the sculptor who gutted the tenement apartment and retrofitted it with shelving, a kitchen, a bed, and closets, Paul has gone on to express his style through a mix of family furnishings and purchased high-concept pieces.

The most impressive feature is the custom-built shelving on one wall that spans the entire length of the apartment. Emphasizing the studio's length, the shelving is a design statement that provides considerable storage and accommodates the kitchen and bed so elegantly that you barely notice them. With so many functions handled by this wall, the other walls could be painted fun colors and lightened up.

Apartments like Paul's pose a challenge when it comes to furniture layout. With a narrow floor plan, it is easy to fill up a room from front to back. Paul decided to cluster the heaviest pieces in the back of the room, in order to keep the front clear. Although the back is crowded, especially when the bed is down, the payoff is a nice open seating area in front of the fireplace in front.

Check out the great closet design. By placing his hanging clothing high, he gains space below for three storage drawers and shoe cubbies by the floor. The way his possessions are separately stored and organized is instantly pleasing.

In this well-appointed tiny apartment, the lessons are all in the nooks and crannies. What you see is driven by problem solving, not just style, and is translatable to any home.

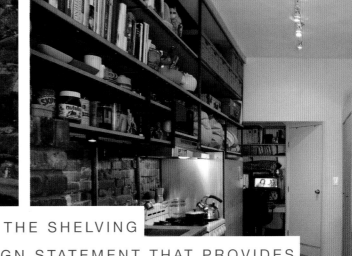

The kitchen is delineated by an eight-foot-long concrete countertop. The counter and the stainless steel sink bring an industrial feel to the historic building.

THE SHELVING IS A DESIGN STATEMENT THAT PROVIDES CONSIDERABLE STORAGE AND ACCOMMODATES THE KITCHEN AND BED...

survey

Style

A mélange of historic features, midcentury modern, and Home Depot industrial.

Inspiration

The efficiency of a train or boat cabin.

Favorite Element

My tall wall of shelves.

Biggest Challenge

Finding a well-built, comfortable small sofa I can fit through the door.

What Friends Say

Really cool.

Biggest Embarrassment

When the Murphy bed is down, the bathroom door can't open all the way. I have to get in by moving sideways.

Proudest DIY

Three Plexi cubes serving as a low bookshelf.

Biggest Indulgence

New Maarten Van Severin .03 chairs. They're sleek, they flex when you sit in them, and they stack.

Best Advice

Economize. I tend to accumulate things, but in this unit, less is more. Keeping this studio clear of clutter is the key to making it feel spacious.

Dream Sources

eBay, flea markets, the bazaars of Istanbul and Morocco.

The high ceilings, storage system, and arrangement of furniture make Paul's apartment feel cozy and comforting rather than claustrophobic. Running along one long wall, the shelving is uniform in design and eliminates the need for freestanding furniture other than seating and decorative pieces. The shelves are made of MDF and steel.

(opposite, top) Paul calls this piece his "nonsofa." It consists of velvet Urban Outfitters *pillows and a divan on top of old industrial pallets made of iron and wood.*

(opposite, bottom) Paul built the Plexiglas *cubes. They rest on three footstools from* Bed Bath & Beyond. *The red table is a traveling shoe-repair box that opens up to reveal an iron shoe rest. Paul keeps his shoe polish and brushes in the box. The sculpture,* Guns and Roses *by* Suck UK, *is from the* ICFF.

The closet built into the wall next to the kitchen has a deep plywood dresser and bifold doors. The apartment is painted in Martha Stewart Everyday Colors *Lady's Mantle and Beach Glass.*

Paul feels it is bad karma to sleep with the bathroom door wide open, but when the Murphy bed is down, the bathroom door doesn't open completely. The horizontally situated Murphy bed makes it possible to fit a full-size sleeping area in the narrow space across from the closet and in front of the home office and bathroom.

The dining room table, custom built for the apartment, has an aluminum top and wooden legs on wheels. The Naugahyde-covered chairs are from Paul's grandmother's basement. A pantry, a liquor cabinet, and a wine rack are built into the wall in front of the table. The lower part of the cabinet accommodates cable and other media and has electrical outlets. Behind the remainder of the wall is a closet for clothes.

An L-shaped section of the wall beyond the dining table can be pulled out to divide the kitchen and bedroom.

(left, bottom) Paul's office is at one end of the apartment, next to the bathroom door and below a large soffit that hides vertical storage.

RESOURCES

BED BATH & BEYOND: bedbathandbeyond.com
HOME DEPOT: homedepot.com
ICFF: www.icff.com
MARTHA STEWART EVERYDAY COLORS: kmart.com
SUCK UK: suck.uk.com
URBAN OUTFITTERS: www.urbanoutfitters.com

30.
raelene and jose's
miami vice

study

sunroom

bedroom

kitchen   **living room**

bathroom

dining room

bedroom

patio

garage

entrance

NAME: RAELENE AND JOSE
PROFESSION: GRAPHIC DESIGNER
(RAELENE) AND COMPTROLLER (JOSE)
LOCATION: MIAMI BEACH
OWNED/RENTED: OWNED
SIZE: 2,200 SQUARE FEET
TYPE: SINGLE-FAMILY RANCH-STYLE HOME
BUILT IN 1939
YEARS LIVED IN: 2

*(opposite) A chandelier designed by
Gino Sarfatti in 1958, a Saarinen
table, and an Eames chair.*

Raelene and Jose were our first house tour in Miami. Through them, we discovered the unique kinship that Miami, town of glitz, shares with New York, town of tinsel. Like many Miami residents, Raelene and Jose left the Northeast to restyle their lives. They brought with them their finely honed design background and set about creating their own interpretation of Miami's open, airy, retro style in a 1930s ranch-style home.

Their first priorities were to give Raelene a comfortable home office and to create a guest room in anticipation of welcoming many visitors. So, to start, they painted everything white – which let them begin with a clean slate. The one area they did not paint was the Earl LePan flamingo mural, the centerpiece of the living room. When Raelene and Jose first saw the house, the seller informed them that the flamingo mural had been painted specifically for the house and intimated that it should remain intact. At first they hated the mural, but now they feel they have seen the light. "Its utter uniqueness and 'Miami-ness,'" Raelene says, "are truly the reason we live here!"

Taking a cue from the mural's centrality to their design philosophy, they decided to refurbish the house – where tropical Mediterranean meets art deco – back to the architect's intentions and then add their own personalities after living in it. Their mantra was: pare away, strip, reduce, and clean. They are still at work and are in no rush to finish.

As they continue to work through their house, they have set their goals high and worked hard to ensure quality, but have avoided a fixed deadline that might stress them out. Passion, artistry, and dedication are more important to them than a rush to the finish. Although not everyone could remain this patient, Raelene and Jose are great examples of the benefits of taking your time and considering every move.

Proudest DIY

Exposing and staining the beams
in the Florida room.

Biggest Indulgence

It will be the kitchen, someday!

Best Advice

Don't rush to finish — the process is
the most enjoyable part (yeah, right).
Don't gut the original quality stuff in
a house and replace it with cheap,
trendy stuff. It will cause someone in
the future to suffer greatly.

Dream Source

Apartment Therapy, of course!

raelene and jose's
survey

Style

A mix of modern and '50s Eames.

Inspiration

All of the other homes we've seen
and loved.

Favorite Elements

The size of the yard and the giant
mango and frangipani trees out
back. The porch renovation — it
meets and greets us every time we
enter the house. We also like the
Earl LePan mural (*Raelene*) and the
ceiling in the "Florida room" (*Jose*).

Biggest Challenge

A previous owner replaced the
nice details with cheaper ones back
in the late '80s. The plans showed
much nicer materials and layout.
Wish we were the owners earlier in
the life of this house!

What Friends Say

It has great bones.

Biggest Embarrassment

Just about everything, as it's
not finished.

*Raelene and Jose have come to love the
mural by Earl LePan. The fireplace is also
an original feature of the 1930s home.
Raelene is slowly designing the living room
around the mural. The long rug from
Luminaire leads from the entry to
the fireplace.*

The cool, modern dining room doesn't have the midcentury feel of the other rooms, but it certainly captures the Miami mood. The walls are painted in Behr's *Tropical Breeze. The chandelier, designed by* Gino Sarfatti *in 1958, is from a* Luminaire *sample sale. A* Batista *folding table is used as an extension of the dining room table for serving food during dinner parties.*

To furnish her office, Raelene coupled a Pottery Barn *metal dining table with a* Herman Miller *Aeron chair. The* Flos *floor lamp is from* Luminaire. *The guest chair is a* Bertoia. IKEA *and the* Container Store *were her sources for bookcases and metal baskets. Raelene inherited the cowhide rug from a friend.*

apartment :: therapy

The guest room (right, top) was one of the first finished rooms. Raelene was looking for an oak bed with a color similar to the midcentury end tables. She found one on Overstock.com. Both the bed and the tables have slightly angled legs. The duvet is by Amenity. The Mibo table lamps are from Design Public, and the wish pillow on the bed is from the W Hotel Store. Raelene discovered the persimmon candlesticks at Sprout Home. The wall behind the bed is painted a custom color of Raelene's invention — a lot of Benjamin Moore's Green Grape and a little Spicy Mustard.

The master bedroom (right) exudes a Miami feel of lightness. The bed and duvet are from CB2, and the comforter is from Target. Raelene bought the regal chair on Craigslist and had it reupholstered. The Philippe Starck Rosy Angelis tripod floor lamp came from a Luminaire sample sale.

(opposite, bottom left) The main hallway down the center of the home has a chair from Wisteria. The Normann-Copenhagen hanging lamp is like a puzzle. It took hours to put the many plastic pieces together.

(opposite, bottom right) Raelene and Jose were determined to update the guest bathroom while restoring its original elements and charm. They removed the sink, mirror, and lights — remnants of a 1980s renovation — and left the bathtub. At a junkyard, Raelene found a sink and toilet that perfectly matched the original bathtub and tiles. The sconces are from Faucet.com's Lighting Showplace, also the source of the Kohler vintage faucet.

Jose painstakingly stripped and refinished the exposed beams in what he and Raelene call the Florida room (left). Removing the old white paint utterly transformed the space. The deep color of the wood provides a dramatic contrast with the white walls and the verdant garden. The tile floor is original. The leather couch is from Luminaire, *and the pillowcase and* Alseda *grass stools are from* IKEA. *The wooden blinds are from* Hunter Douglas.

A corner of the Florida room with views of the garden makes a wonderful dining spot. Raelene found the Saarinen *table,* Eames *chairs, and George Nelson hanging lamp at* retromodern.com.

RESOURCES

AMENITY: amenityhome.com

BEHR: behr.com

BENJAMIN MOORE: benjaminmoore.com

CB2: cb2.com

CONTAINER STORE: containerstore.com

CRAIGSLIST: craigslist.org

DESIGN PUBLIC: designpublic.com

HERMAN MILLER: hermanmiller.com

HUNTER DOUGLAS: hunterdouglas.com

IKEA: ikea.com

LIGHTING SHOWPLACE:

lightingshowplace.com

LUMINAIRE: luminaire.com

NORMANN-COPENHAGEN:

normann-copenhagen.com

OVERSTOCK.COM: overstock.com

POTTERY BARN: potterybarn.com

RETROMODERN: retromodern.com

SPROUT HOME:

store.sprouthome.com

TARGET: target.com

W HOTEL STORE:

whotelsthestore.com

WISTERIA: wisteria.com

photos by
jill slater

31.
robert's
mitchell-lama
labor of love

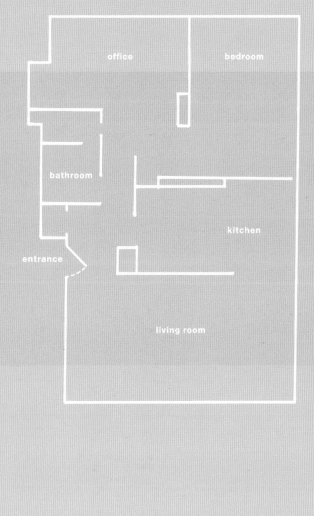

NAME: ROBERT ADAMS
PROFESSION: CITY PLANNER
LOCATION: EAST VILLAGE, NYC
OWNED/RENTED: OWNED
SIZE: 780 SQUARE FEET
TYPE: 2-BEDROOM CO-OP IN A 1960s
MITCHELL-LAMA HIGH-RISE
YEARS LIVED IN: 6

(opposite, left) Most of the walls are painted in Superwhite from **Benjamin Moore**. *Part of the living room wall is blue —"as close to primary blue as we could find," Robert says. The inside of the front door is yellow, also as close to primary as possible. Both oil-based paints are from the Dutch company* **Fine Paints of Europe**.

"Are you building a house in there?"
asks Blanche, Robert's elderly neighbor,
when she sees him schlep construction materials

down the hall week after week. Blanche has known Robert since 1964, the year he was born—the same year that these Mitchell-Lama apartments were completed and the same year that Robert's grandparents moved out of their tenement on the Lower East Side and into their spacious affordable apartment in this modern high-rise.

All of this makes Robert a special breed of DIY pioneer. Among the few that are willing to move back home, he was ready, willing, and able to renovate the interior like a pro, turning it into a high-end design statement. Unlike many of the homes in this book, this is a fancy apartment, and the word *budget* has not been applied. However, Robert did do much of the work himself, and there is a lot to learn.

All of the Mitchell-Lama apartments in NYC were built by the city as co-ops for the middle class—a concept that is almost hard to fathom in the current real-estate development madness. Because the apartments were meant to be part of a large cooperative, current owners are restricted from selling their units on the open market. Therefore, Robert leapt at the opportunity to take over the apartment when his grandparents died. He knew he was going to make it his long-term home.

All of the original elements were intact: fully enclosed boxy rooms, rich green carpeting, deep beige walls, and sea foam/gray bathroom motif. Robert immediately began renovating while living in the space. The project has taken three years and is not entirely finished.

Robert designed and/or built many of the new features: the wall unit in the living room, the shelving in the bedroom and study, the desk, the kitchen cabinets (with doors from IKEA), the countertop, and the medicine cabinet. If Robert doesn't get your own DIY wheels turning (or inspire a desire for cork floors), nothing will.

Robert designed and built the shelving unit for the area adjacent to the kitchen. The dishes, called Teema, are made by Iittala *in Finland. Robert bought them over an eight-year period from a now-closed SoHo store, on the Internet, and at* Zabar's. *The rest of the tableware comes from* Fishs Eddy.

The dining room table and chairs (far left) are Danish modern. The table is from Modernlink, *and the chairs are from* Las Venus. *The chairs were reupholstered by* Gerard Theuns *in Brooklyn, who carries* Marjam/Kvadrat *wool fabrics from Denmark in an array of colors. The floor is laid with* Aronson's *cork tile. The cork, made by* Wicanders *in Portugal, is "cooked" (not dyed) to achieve the brown color. In different parts of the house, Robert used polyurethane or wax to seal the tiles.*

The Boontje *light covering (left) is from* Moss.

robert's
survey

Style

I am trying to create a style that goes well with the 1960s concrete boxiness of our low-ceiling apartment but is also warm and inviting and not too dated.

Inspiration

I am inspired by modernist interiors primarily because they suit this particular apartment so well — but I am drawn to the tasteful mixing of old and new that can be found in journals such as *The World of Interiors.*

Favorite Element

The wide window blinds, which have done so much to "deinstitutionalize" the institutional apartment and yet are in keeping with its aesthetic.

Biggest Challenge

The biggest challenge is to introduce warmer, eclectic, decorative elements. It seems much easier to add minimalist or modernist touches to older houses that already have details such as moldings, window frames, or hardwood floors. My aim is to do the reverse, i.e., add detail to an apartment that does not welcome it easily.

What Friends Say

Friends and relatives are usually (favorably) shocked if they knew this apartment "before" and know what I started with.

Biggest Embarrassment

The ongoing lack of practicality. Our most recent example: very dark brown, low-pile carpeting that appears to attract bits of dust just seconds after it is vacuumed. But I love it.

Proudest DIY

The bookshelves in the living room. They're a bit crooked here and there, but this magically does not show! And I am enjoying filling them and developing their presence and personality.

Biggest Indulgence

The bathroom fixtures were a pricey splurge.

Best Advice

Have the interior completely gutted (including all nonstructural walls) and start with a blank slate. Nearly all our design struggles have come from contending with the original layout, which is full of strange corners, projections, and walls that don't align.

Dream Source

I make many inspirational treks to John Derian off Bond Street, but have yet to figure out a way to make any of his beautiful objects fit into the house.

(left) The red **Eames** *chair is from* **Design Within Reach.** *The couch, covered in a* **Knoll** *fabric, is a convertible from* **Carlyle Sofa.**

Robert's proudest DIY achievement is the white-painted plywood wall unit (below). He is happy with both the scale and the proportions. The Italian lamp was a wedding gift.

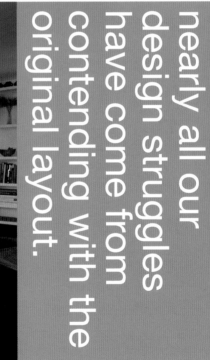

nearly all our design struggles have come from contending with the original layout.

Robert designed and built all the shelving and installed a strip of lights along the upper rear edge of each module. The blinds are wider than the windows, giving the illusion that the room receives more natural light than it actually does. The carpet, from Aronson's, *is a brown short-pile wool carpet with an extra layer of wool below to create thickness without the cost of a high-pile rug.*

The blue tile is by Bisazza. *The sink and toilet are by* Duravit. *The bathroom fixtures are* Tara *by* Dornbracht. *The fluorescent light is from* Artemide.

Robert designed the medicine cabinet and then built out the recessed frame that would hold it. He gave his drawings to Canal Plastics, *which fabricated the plastic interior.*

RESOURCES

The gray tile on the backsplash is by Bisazza. *Robert bought the* Arne Jacobsen *kitchen faucet at* David Sanders *on the Bowery. The stainless steel counter was fabricated and then wrapped over a wooden counter that he had cut at* Bowery Building Supply. *The door pulls are from* Design Source, *and the refrigerator is* GE.

ARONSON'S: aronsonsfloors.com

ARTEMIDE: artemide.com

BENJAMIN MOORE: benjaminmoore.com

BISAZZA: bisazzausa.com

BOWERY BUILDING SUPPLY: 212.505.0022

CANAL PLASTICS: canalplasticscenter.com

CARLYLE SOFA: carlylesofa.com

DESIGN SOURCE: designsourceltd.com

DESIGN WITHIN REACH: dwr.com

DORNBRACHT: dornbracht.com

FINE PAINTS OF EUROPE:

finepaintsofeurope.com

FISHS EDDY: fishseddy.com

GE: geappliances.com

GERARD THEUNS: 718.237.4619

IITTALA: iittala.com

JOHN DERIAN DRY GOODS:

johnderian.com

KNOLL: knoll.com

LAS VENUS: lasvenus.com

MODERNLINK: modernlink.com

MOSS: mossonline.com

WICANDERS: wicanders.com

WORLD OF INTERIORS:

worldofinteriors.co.uk/

ZABAR'S: zabars.com

photos by
**maxwell
gillingham-ryan**

32.

sara kate and maxwell's gourmet shoe box

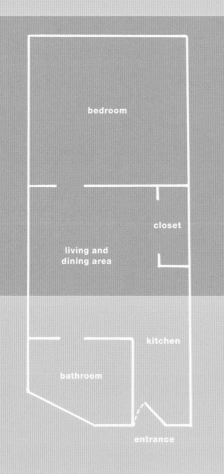

NAME: SARA KATE AND MAXWELL GILLINGHAM-RYAN

PROFESSION: FOOD WRITER (SARA KATE) AND INTERIOR DESIGNER/BLOGGER (MAXWELL)

LOCATION: WEST VILLAGE, NYC

OWNED/RENTED: RENTED

SIZE: 265 SQUARE FEET

TYPE: GROUND-FLOOR APARTMENT IN A 4-STORY RESIDENCE BUILT IN 1904

YEARS LIVED IN: 14

The new galley kitchen (opposite, left) is just inside the front door. The counter is one piece of Durat recycled polymer, which is 100 percent recyclable. The track lights are simple, inexpensive white metal fixtures with halogen bulbs. The five-inch-wide oak flooring is stained a dark chocolate brown and sealed with water-based polyurethane.

This apartment stands as a beacon of hope for all those who feel that their home is too small or too ugly ever to be reclaimed. Apartment Therapy began in this studio twelve years ago when I traded apartments with my girlfriend at the time. She was sick of the dingy, ground-floor unit and wanted a bigger, brighter place. Meanwhile, I had been sharing a two-bedroom apartment and wanted my own place. Moving into my first solo apartment in NYC at the age of twenty-eight, I immediately went to work by taking out all the doors (including the bathroom door), removing as much furniture as possible, and painting all the dark trim white.

Three subsequent renovations later, this is still my favorite apartment in the world, and it comfortably houses our family of three. We have very nice landlords who patiently stood by as we slowly and systematically changed almost everything about the apartment to suit our needs. In our latest and biggest renovation, which was preparation for baby Ursula, we removed and replaced the bathroom, kitchen, and half of the floor. The new kitchen makes the best use of the space and allows Sara Kate to cook professionally at home. We upgraded the bathroom by retiling it and adding new fixtures. And we skim-coated and repainted the walls and ceiling to create a feeling of newness and calm. We had the help of a contractor this time, but all the finishing touches are DIY.

This last project was a hair-raiser. Two months before Ursula's birth, we ran into multiple difficulties, and the contractors didn't finish until the day after we left for the hospital. Sara Kate's mother likes to remind me that she had to cover up piles of tools with white sheets just to make the apartment look nice when Sara Kate started going into labor at home.

It was a tremendous amount of work, but it all got done. The major features are a spacious, environmentally conscious kitchen from Henrybuilt, a wide-plank oak floor stained dark to ground the kitchen space, and a number of beautiful fixtures that were not cheap but work flawlessly and will be usable for a long, long time. "But how long will you stay in your studio with a baby," you ask? This being expensive NYC and a neighborhood we love, we'll stay as long as we can, and then keep the apartment as an office and guest house for our West Coast family.

Having open storage space for cups and plates was important to us. Henrybuilt *made the shelves as thick as the cabinets. The undersides have built-in LED lights to illuminate the sink area.*

"This apartment
stands
as a beacon
of hope
for all those
who feel
that their home
is too small
or too ugly
ever to be
reclaimed."

sara kate and maxwell's
survey

Style

We think we're modern, but when we look around there are a lot of traditional influences. We like it to be cozy, light-filled, and not cluttered. Natural is also important. With our garden outside and cut flowers and compost inside, we try to bring in as much nature as possible. Let's say we're organic modern.

Inspiration

The space itself. We've just pared it down until it's as simple as it gets. We've also been inspired by all of the homes we've seen at Apartment Therapy over the years.

Favorite Elements

If forced to pick, we would say our new kitchen, which has transformed our cooking, and our bedroom storage, which is easy to get at, bright, and all we need.

Biggest Challenge

Trying to fit a living room, dining room, and kitchen into one room and not make it too crowded.

What Friends Say

"Oh, how beautiful . . . but, seriously, when are you going to move?"

Biggest Embarrassment

Our garden! During the renovation it got trashed. It used to be beautiful, and it now needs a lot of work.

Proudest DIY

Our white felt doors. This was an idea we had many years ago. The renovation gave us the opportunity to test felts and tracks, and made us spend the money to pull it off. It works better than expected.

Biggest Indulgence

The Dornbracht faucet in the bathroom. It was quite expensive, but we use it constantly and really, really appreciate it.

Best Advice

Less is more. It's something we say to ourselves all the time and it's always true.

Dream Source

Paris for eclectic, beautiful vintage finds, BDDW for furniture, and Troy for seating.

Our humble dining room had to be perfect for two and expandable for four. We chose a round table and two dreamy Cherner chairs in deep red. The curtains are from Pottery Barn. The mirror is from an antique store and the lamp from our family.

(opposite) The stove was important, and we spent a good deal of time checking our options in twenty-four-inch cook tops and ovens. The Delonghi cook top won by a long shot. We chose a Delonghi gas oven as well, because our apartment can't handle another major electrical appliance. The kitchen wall was painted with Nacho Cheese by Benjamin Moore. The quarter-inch-thick glass backstop is easily cleanable and was inspired by seeing Cedric Devit's similar solution for his kitchen.

The kitchen was designed and built by Henrybuilt to our specs out of solid bamboo, a sustainable material. We now have four times more storage than in our old kitchen. The stainless steel sink is from Just Sinks, and the faucet is a Blanco Merkur S. The small Summit Built-in Fridge Freezer is from Compact Appliance.

When we gutted the bathroom (opposite, top left), we kept only the tub and the toilet. The ten-inch shower head is from Charles Taylor Specialties. We bought the remaining fixtures at Simon's Hardware: Dornbracht Meta 0.2 faucet and glass shelf, Robern cabinet, Vitra sink, and Sine Motiv sconces. The Capriccio subway tile in antique white is from Ann Sacks. Our favorite shower curtain is from Matouk.

Having a good place to hang towels in the bathroom is a must (opposite, top right). The hooks are from Restoration Hardware. Wrapping the hot-water pipe in manila rope from a marina makes it cool to the touch. The bathroom color is Pale Avocado by Benjamin Moore.

Our bed (above) fits perfectly between storage units, which become bedside tables. The Sonno mattress is from Design Within Reach. The wall color is Lambs-wool by Benjamin Moore.

Maxwell custom-built the bedroom features (right), drawing inspiration from a friend, Marre Moerel, who invented the box system illuminated from within. All cabinet and counter-top surfaces are wrapped in white Naugahyde from Knoll. The linen curtains are from Pottery Barn. The wall shelving is Elfa from the Container Store.

The felt doors (above, left) make our space dividable, but don't take up room. They were inspired by Morgan Puett's supercool 1980s shop, which was all done in industrial felt. We bought the half-inch-thick white felt from Sutherland Felt *and mounted it to the ceiling with hospital track painted white. The grips are made from thick raw leather.*

To maximize the storage in our only closet (above, right), we used Astech Closets *to install this custom design that evenly splits the space in two. Our biggest piece of furniture is a Sleepytime rocker by* Nurseryworks, *purchased at* Design Public. *The side table is from* IKEA. *The painting is by Maxwell, copied from a print he saw in a* Kate Spade *store.*

RESOURCES

ANN SACKS:
annsacks.com

ASTECH CLOSETS:
astechclosets.com

BENJAMIN MOORE:
benjaminmoore.com

CHARLES TAYLOR SPECIALTIES:
212-226-5369

CHERNER CHAIR CO.:
chernerchair.com

COMPACT APPLIANCE:
compactappliance.com

CONTAINER STORE:
thecontainerstore.com

DELONGHI: delonghi.com

DESIGN PUBLIC:
designpublic.com

DESIGN WITHIN REACH:
designwithinreach.com

DORNBRACHT:
dornbracht.com

DURAT: durat.com

FISHS EDDY:
fishseddy.com

HENRYBUILT:
henrybuilt.com

JUST SINKS:
justsinks.com

IKEA: ikea.com

KNOLL: knoll.com

MARRE MOEREL:
marremoerel.com

MATOUK: matouk.com

NURSERYWORKS:
nurseryworks.net

POTTERY BARN:
potterybarn.com

RESTORATION HARDWARE:
restorationhardware.com

ROBERN: robern.com

SIMON'S HARDWARE:
simons-hardware.com

SUTHERLAND FELT CO.:
sutherlandfelt.com

VITRA: vitra.com

photos by
evan thomas

33.
shannon and emmett's
from factory to family

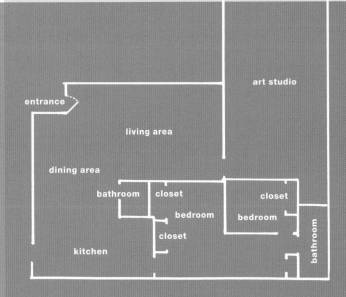

art studio

entrance

living area

dining area

bathroom closet closet

bedroom bedroom

closet

kitchen bathroom

NAME: SHANNON AND EMMETT KERRIGAN
PROFESSION: ARTISTS
LOCATION: RIVER WEST, CHICAGO
OWNED/RENTED: OWNED
SIZE: 1,700-SQ-FOOT APARTMENT
AND 1,500-SQ-FOOT STUDIO
TYPE: 2-BEDROOM APARTMENT
AND ART STUDIO IN 1920s
INDUSTRIAL BUILDING
YEARS LIVED IN: 14

Shannon and Emmett's magnificent home, our first Chicago house tour, made all the New Yorkers jealous with its deliciously huge industrial space. The real lesson here is that it's possible to create comfort and beauty in an expansive industrial environment.

In 1993 Emmett and his brother bought an abandoned powder-coating factory in Chicago's River West neighborhood. Being artists, they were up for a challenge and decided to try their hand at demo, carpentry, plumbing, drywall, and myriad other tasks in order to create studio space for themselves. Shannon, a sculptor and Emmett's wife, joined them after a few years and soon was making her own design contributions. Over a decade later, the project is complete. Each of the family members has a large work space in addition to their independent two-bedroom loft-style apartment. Additional cooperative studio space contains welding facilities and kilns.

Shannon and Emmett's apartment has exposed brick, heavy timber beams, and huge windows along one wall. The main open space serves as kitchen, dining room, and living room. The two bedrooms and bathrooms are enclosed areas, as is the painting studio. Skylights and repurposed windows set high into the interior walls let natural light into the back rooms.

As you tour their home, you will come upon enviable ideas and finds such as the butter-yellow metal kitchen cabinets and stainless cook top from a retired cabinetmaker in Indiana. In one room, a small computer work space and bookshelves cleverly made from salvaged stair treads are used along a wall. Spread throughout are collections of pottery, quirky toys, found curiosities, and artwork by Emmett, Shannon, and their friends, all of which give their home its distinct character.

IT'S POSSIBLE TO CREATE COMFORT AND BEAUTY IN AN EXPANSIVE INDUSTRIAL ENVIRONMENT.

shannon and emmett's
survey

Style

Modern eclectic.

Inspiration

Our parents are really into interior design, so we absorbed some wisdom from them, and then "we just did it."

Favorite Elements

Douglas fir timber ceilings and yellow enameled steel kitchen cabinets from the '50s.

Biggest Challenge

Deciding which space would be for living and which would be for work.

What Friends Say

They like the art.

Biggest Embarrassment

Powder room is still unfinished.

Proudest DIY

Laying the floors and hanging the drywall.

Biggest Indulgence

Our modern furniture collection.

Best Advice

Art studio comes first, so make sure to leave room for it.

Dream Source

Modern Times in Chicago.

The living space (top) has both a breakfast area and a main dining table. Hanging above the white Eames table and four red chairs from Modern Times is a lamp that Shannon found at Salvation Army. Three Italian glass lamps hang above the Knoll dining table and Herman Miller chairs purchased at Urban Artifacts. The dining table centerpiece is a hand-blown glass cloche made by a friend.

This corner of the living room is for both relaxing and playing. The comfy leather reading chairs and ottoman are from Marshall Fields. The toy suspended from the ceiling is a horse made from recycled tires. Hanging on the wall are Emmett's tricycle paintings.

A vintage metal office credenza holds some of Emmett's wooden sculptures. The vintage lamp is one of a pair purchased at Modern Times. Emmett's paintings of fans hang on the wall, which separates the living space and the art studio.

Emmett found the 1950s metal kitchen cabinets through an ad. The original prototypes were installed in the cabinet designer's own home and are in perfect condition. Displayed on top of the cabinets is a collection of Haeger pottery. The hanging lamp was in the space when Emmett purchased it. He kept a few of the factory lamps and repainted them. The stool is vintage Knoll, and the barware was made by a friend.

The bedroom receives light from the main space through the windows above the bed. Metal night-stands from Maxwell Street hold vintage lamps purchased from different sources. The sofa is from Herman Miller. The shelf holds a series of light boxes made from four-by-five slides of Emmett's paintings. A painting by Emmett hangs on the wall. The window above the desk looks into their son's room.

Shannon and Emmett designed the desk (top left) and adjacent shelving and built the pieces from salvaged stair treads and threaded rods from Home Depot. *The desk chair is a* Herman Miller *from* Urban Artifacts. *The large carpet, which covers much of the floor in the living area, is a* William Morris *pattern. Shannon bought it new on* eBay. *The wall relief consists of nine large tiles from the* Bryan Kerrigan Tile Co.

The vintage metal apothecary cabinet (top right) holds all sorts of treasures. A similar cabinet stands nearby. One came from a garage sale, the other from Modern Times.

Two Saarinen *dressers (above, left) are set up side by side against the exposed brick wall in the bedroom. The dressers and the* Alexander Calder *print on the wall came from a* John Toomey Auction. *The turntable, a custom piece by* Juan Chavez, *is made from salvaged wood and vintage components.*

This is the younger Emmett's room (above, right). The bunk bed is from Marshall Fields. *The kites on the wall were bought at a flea market. The framed print by* Tony Fitzpatrick *is from a show at the Chicago* Museum of Contemporary Art. *Shannon got the two wall-hung beta bowls from* PetsMart.

Spread throughout are collections of pottery,
quirky toys, found curiosities, and artwork . . . .
which give their home its distinct character.

The studio receives lots of natural light from the skylights that run the length of the space. The paintings and wooden tops are Emmett's work. The metal wall sculptures and reclining figure are Shannon's.

RESOURCES

BRYAN KERRIGAN TILE CO.: kerriganart.com
CHICAGO MUSEUM OF CONTEMPORARY ART:
mcachicago.org
EBAY: ebay.com
EMMETT KERRIGAN: emmettart.com
HAEGER: haegerpotteries.com
HERMAN MILLER: hermanmiller.com
HOME DEPOT: homedepot.com
JUAN CHAVEZ: juanangelchavez.com
JOHN TOOMEY AUCTIONS: treadwaygallery.com
KNOLL: knoll.com
MARSHALL FIELDS: fields.com
MODERN TIMES: moderntimeschicago.com
PETSMART: petsmart.com
SALVATION ARMY: salvationarmy.org
URBAN ARTIFACTS: 773.404.1008

photos by
shauna cross

34.
shauna and fred's
more dash than cash

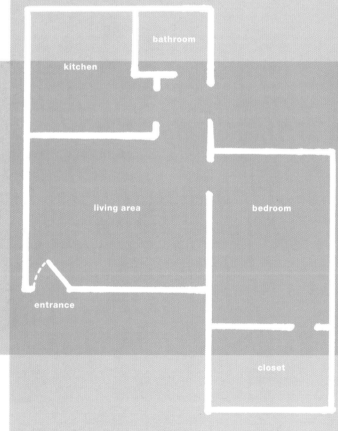

bathroom

kitchen

living area

bedroom

entrance

closet

NAME: SHAUNA CROSS AND FRED JASPER
PROFESSION: SCREENWRITER (SHAUNA)
AND AUTHOR (FRED)
LOCATION: HANCOCK PARK, LA
OWNED/RENTED: RENTED
SIZE: 636 SQUARE FEET
TYPE: 1-BEDROOM IN A 1920s FOURPLEX
YEARS LIVED IN: 2 YEARS

Shauna has created real glamour on a budget without any catalog clichés in sight.

Her eclectic mix brings back a slice of Americana in a fresh way. Despite her love of vintage furnishings, the apartment is not cluttered or cloying because a strong sense of organization lies behind everything. It isn't just style that makes an impression; it is also structure. Old album covers are perfectly framed and centered above a bar; impeccable standing files sit in a tidy home office; nine French soap bars are neatly stacked inside a glass urn in the bathroom; and a crisp, wide stripe runs midway around the living room and hallway walls. Shauna may not have spent a lot of money, but she definitely spent a good deal of time — and it shows.

Which is our favorite room? It has to be the shiny pear-green living room. The layout is near perfect and a showcase for our theory of three-point seating. Most living rooms are oriented toward the television and lack enough seating to make them social centers. To create a welcoming living room, you want at least three points of seating that face one another — typically two chairs and a sofa. This is exactly what Shauna has here. Her elegant slipper chairs are turned away from the television to face the sofa, forming a social circle that is further emphasized by the round coffee table and rug.

Take time to notice Shauna's excellent use of color. Although her color palette may not be your taste, each room works harmoniously, with no color out of place, and the variation from room to room creates nice spatial separation. When you don't have a great deal of square footage, this kind of variation gives a feeling of spaciousness.

Shauna's kitchen is so small that she felt it was more worthwhile to put a bar (left) in the room instead of a dining table. She found this 1950s piece on eBay. Shauna considers herself a gutsy eBay user. She rarely buys anything for over $150 and knows she can always sell it for at least what she paid for it. The plates are 1960s turquoise melamine. The vintage glasses have a travel theme. The 1950s bark cloth drapes are from Out of the Closet, *and the bamboo floor mat is from* Crate & Barrel.

Victorian butterfly plates (above) hang in the hallway.

Style

Vintage modern awesome (*Shauna*). Shauna's the driving force behind the decorating in our apartment, but we both adhere to the philosophy of surrounding yourself with things that you love. Fortunately, we love a lot of the same things (*Fred*).

Inspiration

'20s art deco, '30s screen sirens, the atomic '50s, old movies, music, and laughter — high culture mingling with low culture. Our home is casual, colorful, and friendly.

Favorite Elements

Old butterfly plates and a carved wood stool that Fred gave me (*Shauna*). Early in the courting of Shauna, she introduced me to her matching lime-green mohair chairs. I still love them. Also, the decorative owl from the late '60s we rescued from a West Virginia antique mall. We named him "Monroe" (*Fred*).

Biggest Challenge

Making it work for two people and dinner parties for eight (sans dining room and with an itty-bitty kitchen!).

What Friends Say

It's completely original, calm, and full of cool stuff without being cluttered. And "Wow! Where'd you get that [insert apartment object here]?"

Biggest Embarrassment

The bathroom is the size of a postage stamp. If you sit on the toilet, your knees hit the wall.

Proudest DIY

The chalk mural on the bedroom wall. It was going to be a mural to echo the look of chinoiserie wallpaper (on a budget), but the sketch looked so cool, we decided to leave it as is and not paint it in.

Biggest Indulgence

Flat-screen, hi-def TV (we heart our new fancy TV — is that shallow?), taffeta drapes from the Silk Trading Company (they make a room full of flea market furniture look like a million bucks), fresh flowers, artisan cheeses, and imported dark chocolate.

Best Advice

Let your place tell the story of who lives there — that never goes out of style. The best and most soulful interiors are those that evolve over time.

Dream Source

Paris flea markets, anything from Firstdibs.com, or a time machine to go back and collect the best from different eras (*Shauna*). A relative I didn't know (*Fred*).

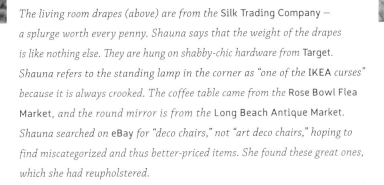

The living room drapes (above) are from the **Silk Trading Company** —
a splurge worth every penny. Shauna says that the weight of the drapes
is like nothing else. They are hung on shabby-chic hardware from **Target**.
Shauna refers to the standing lamp in the corner as "one of the **IKEA** curses"
because it is always crooked. The coffee table came from the **Rose Bowl Flea
Market**, and the round mirror is from the **Long Beach Antique Market**.
Shauna searched on **eBay** for "deco chairs," not "art deco chairs," hoping to
find miscategorized and thus better-priced items. She found these great ones,
which she had reupholstered.

The living room paint scheme (right) continues down both sides of the
hallway leading to the bathroom. Shauna's source for good inexpensive
artwork is **gigposters.com**.

(opposite) The credenza is from the **Rose Bowl Flea Market**. Shauna found
the **Bertoia** chairs in an alley. With a little cleaning and some **Cost Plus**
cushions, they were as good as new. Shauna painted the living room three
shades of beige, with the two lightest shades on the top and bottom.

In the bedroom, Shauna painted the wall and then sketched the bird in a tree with chalk. She decided not to paint the image and not to seal the wall, and says that it is doing fine as is. The headboard is from Overstock.com. The bolster pillows are from Target.

The two dressers are from IKEA. Placing them alongside one another makes them look customized rather than generic. Shauna generally finds brand-name items like this zebra rug online for a third of the price charged in the stores in her neighborhood.

(left) Shauna and Fred use the patio a lot, especially since the apartment doesn't have a dining room table. She hung the gauze to create an intimate enclosure. The chairs and table are 1940s garden furniture from the Rose Bowl Flea Market.

Below are original sketches from a New Orleans lingerie shop. Shauna found them at an antique mall in Texas. She had them framed for the bedroom.

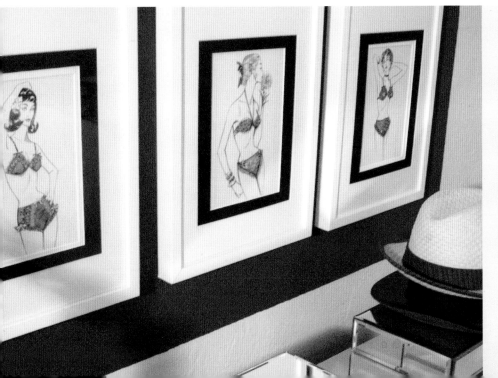

RESOURCES

COST PLUS WORLD MARKET: worldmarket.com

CRATE & BARREL: crateandbarrel.com

EBAY: ebay.com

FIRSTDIBS.COM: 1stdibs.com

GIGPOSTERS: gigposters.com

IKEA: ikea.com

LONG BEACH ANTIQUE MARKET: longbeachantiquemarket.com

OUT OF THE CLOSET: outofthecloset.org

OVERSTOCK.COM: overstock.com

ROSE BOWL FLEA MARKET: rosebowlstadium.com/rosebowl_fleamarket.htm

SILK TRADING COMPANY: silktrading.com

TARGET: target.com

photos by
thom finan

35.

thom's san fran delight

living area

bedroom

closet

dining area

entrance

bathroom   closet

kitchen

NAME: THOM FINAN
PROFESSION: RETIRED EXECUTIVE
VICE PRESIDENT
LOCATION: MISSION DISTRICT,
SAN FRANCISCO
OWNED/RENTED: OWNED
SIZE: 640 SQUARE FEET
TYPE: 1-BEDROOM IN AN EARLY-1980s
APARTMENT BUILDING
YEARS LIVED IN: 21

(opposite) The mirrors installed on a number of walls (left) make the space look much larger than it is. Thom bought the custom-made white chair (right) on Craigslist from its original owner. He was struck by its unusual scale. The round coffee table from the 1970s had a brass finish that Thom repainted silver and black. The artwork is a copy of a well-known Picasso painting by an Atlanta artist. Thom spends most of his time in this part of the apartment. He designed and installed the birch wall to add warmth to the room. He also designed and built the mirrored cabinet, which holds

Variety is the spice of life, and Thom's apartment is very spicy.

We love how daring he is with decor. No matter how hesitant people are to use color, there is no doubt that color makes us happy. Thom's story is inspirational. Adding color was, for him, a way of recovering from the depression following his partner's death in 2001. For a long time, this space had been "very Zen," he says, and very plain. Now it feels positively rich.

Many people living in small apartments use muted colors to enlarge the space; Thom has gone the opposite way. In addition to using strong colors, he intermittently injects white to balance the whole equation. One white element plays a major role: the curtains. As floor-to-ceiling fixtures, they become a wall of white that brightens up the ends of every room and reflects a lot of light into the interior.

Look closely at the cleverly hidden lighting. Thom has tucked colored Christmas lights in the molding near the ceiling in the main living space and inserted rope lights behind the beech panel he attached to the side walls. Indirect light streams out of these crevices and gives the space a warm, cozy feeling. As Thom says, the effect is "much like that of a fireplace, without having the maintenance of one."

We love how daring he is with decor.

his art supplies and tools. The 1950s desk lamp is a Lisa Johansson-Pape *from a thrift store. The luxurious chaise, covered in an animal pelt, has down-filled silk and cashmere pillows.*

*Thom's dining area (above) feels
expansive thanks to the wall of mirrors. He built the banquette to cre-
ate more seating in the constrained space. The vintage velvet dining/office
chair is by* **Ward Bennett Design.** *Thom bought the fishbowl at a local
thrift store and turned it into a vase. The vintage Lucite chandelier was
just a pile of pieces in a box at an LA flea market. Thom took a gamble and
invested the $10. When he got home and put it together, he was thrilled.*

Thom made the metal wall (right) with small galvanized steel panels from
Home Depot. *By screwing them at the corners, he created a tufted effect
that enhances the light-reflective quality. Thom loves how the wall helps
illuminate the whole room.*

The kitchen looks large because of the mirrors at the end of the room. The hanging object is the shell of a model boat from a thrift store. Thom likes that it suggests tribal art.

The original cabinets had a walnut stain. Thom prefers cherry, so he created a burled wood effect using a piece of striated cardboard to apply dark cherry stain. The floating box above the sink is a wooden CD holder that Thom painted burnt orange. The fruit bowls came from thrift stores.

thom's
survey

Style

"Eclectique."

Inspiration

Designer Kelly Wearstler.

Favorite Element

The mirrored walls.

Biggest Challenge

Creating vignettes while not making it look cluttered.

What Friends Say

They say that it is warm, sexy, and beautiful.

Biggest Embarrassment

Don't look in the closets.

Proudest DIY

That would be my seven-foot-tall by three-foot-wide slanted metal wall located in my dining area that I created with rectangular pieces of sheet metal, screws, and grommets from Home Depot.

Biggest Indulgence

The birch walls.

Best Advice

Buy things you love that speak to you, not by price point.

Dream Source

Any place that sells things that are out of the ordinary.

(below, top) Thom designed the pillow with fabric he brought back from Florence, Italy. The art glass on the small bedside table was a gift from Monument Furniture & Décor.

(below, bottom) Thom designed the birch headboard that runs the entire width of the bedroom, creating a nice clean line. The blue leather chair is from Craigslist. *The lamp, also from* Craigslist, *is a signed piece by* Sascha Brastoff. *He couldn't find a night table of the right height, so he built one. The three leather baskets serve as mini-drawers. Thom's best friend designed and built the mosaic tile top to mimic the curves of the bookcase.*

IN ADDITION TO USING STRONG COLORS, HE INTERMITTENTLY INJECTS WHITE TO BALANCE THE WHOLE EQUATION.

(opposite, top right) An avid collector, Thom needed a place to store and display his treasures, so he built this undulating bookcase for his bedroom. He wanted the shape to suggest ocean waves.

RESOURCES

CRAIGSLIST: craigslist.org

HOME DEPOT: homedepot.com

JONATHAN ADLER: jonathanadler.com

MONUMENT FURNITURE & DÉCOR: 415.861.9800

(below) Thom has always enjoyed collecting glass and recently became interested in white pottery. He found everything in thrift stores, except the small textured **Jonathan Adler** *vase (below), a gift from a friend.*

photos by
**susanna
friedrich**

36.
todd and nicole's project precita

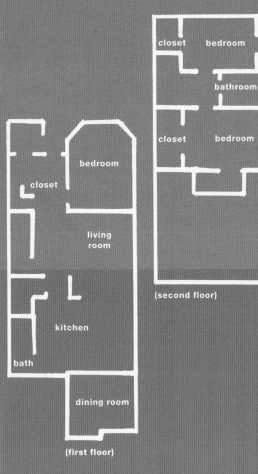

NAME: TODD AND NICOLE

PROFESSION: JOURNALIST (TODD)

AND NONPROFIT ARTS ADMINISTRATOR (NICOLE)

LOCATION: BERNAL HEIGHTS, SAN FRANCISCO

OWNED/RENTED: OWNED

SIZE: 1,800 SQUARE FEET

TYPE: VICTORIAN-ERA SINGLE-FAMILY HOME

YEARS LIVED IN: 2

closet

bedroom

bathroom

closet

bedroom

(second floor)

bedroom

closet

living
room

kitchen

bath

dining room

(first floor)

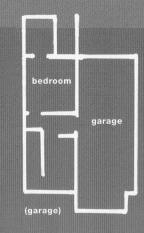

bedroom

garage

(garage)

modern, and also inviting,
warm, and surprising in its reuse of
commercial materials.

Never have we seen a home that is at once so elegant and so devoted to midcentury metallic artifacts. Todd and Nicole bought this modest home on a San Francisco hill and immediately began by gutting the house and undertaking two years of painstaking reconstruction before they officially moved in. The result is very modern, and also inviting, warm, and surprising in its reuse of commercial materials.

The exterior is painted an unusual color – one that closely approximates the Golden Gate Bridge. The inside of the home contains a mélange of rescued artifacts from California's closed military bases, accessories adapted from trucking catalogs, high-tech features, utilitarian objects, and original art.

Of particular note are the stripped and backlit airplane fuselage on one wall and the two large doors that Todd and Nicole built from wooden doors, aluminum panels, and industrial sliding-door track. These features are perfect examples of the rough industrial pieces that find balance against the more common homey elements, such as the warm brown floors, rugs, and upholstered furniture. The juxtaposition gives their home its vitality.

Scavenging, or "antiquing" as it might more politely be called, finds a new level of intensity in Todd and Nicole's house, and we think that the ideas they executed in this remodel are inspiring. Whether or not you are a nut for old military and industrial artifacts, their home will give you fresh ideas.

The backlit chunk of a Boeing 707 fuselage is the first thing you see upon entering Todd and Nicole's home and is one of the many surprises. Todd purchased it at a Tucson aircraft scrap yard for $350 and shipped it to San Francisco for $150. He stripped the paint down to the bare aluminum and wired the fuselage with inexpensive rope lights.

todd and nicole's
survey

Style

Contemporary modernism meets
the military-industrial complex.

Inspiration

The open layouts of Frank Lloyd
Wright, the broken ruins of the former
Hunters Point Naval Shipyard, the
converted army barracks at the
Headlands Center for the Arts, and the
Golden Gate Bridge.

Favorite Element

Our solution for mounting the
flat-panel TV.

Biggest Challenge

Surviving to see the project completed.
We were incredibly naive about what
it would take to renovate our home,
and made just about every mistake
possible. Our first contractor was a
bozo, and we had to fire him. We
underbudgeted. We underestimated
how much time it would take. But
as we often reminded one another during the darkest of those days, "Failure
was not an option."

What Friends Say

They usually say two things. First,
"Wow, I would've never guessed based
on the look of the house from the
outside!" Then, "Nicole, you must be
very, very tolerant." (She is.)

Biggest Embarrassment

None so far, but time will tell!

Proudest DIY

The living room media rack.

Biggest Indulgence

The accordion folding doors, from
Nana Wall Systems, that open wide to
allow circulation between the dining
room and the outside patio.

Best Advice

You can have it done well, quickly, or
cheaply, but you can only pick two.

Dream Source

Boeing, the U.S. Navy, and NASA.

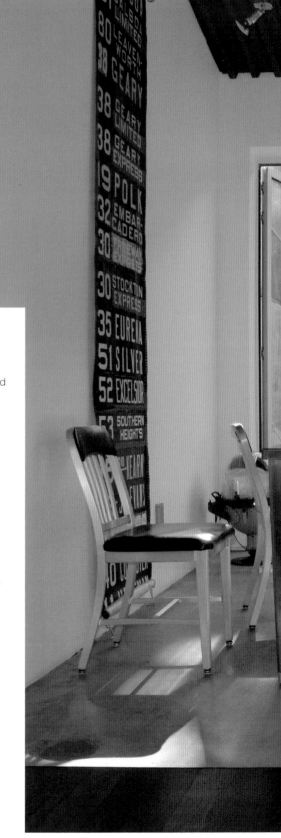

The large patio doors, from **Nana Wall Systems**, open effortlessly onto the backyard and are impervious to wind and weather. Steel decking from **Dek-Ing** is screwed into the ceiling rafters above the dining room and kitchen. Todd wanted to paint it, as well as the facade of the house, the precise color of the Golden Gate Bridge. He learned that Fireweed (SW 6328) by **Sherwin-Williams** was the closest color available to consumers. Most of the lighting in the kitchen is made from utilitarian electrical conduit. Residential LED lighting was too expensive, so he adapted LED lights for tow trucks and service vehicles, purchased from **AW Direct**.

Todd and Nicole originally planned to put a gas fireplace here (below, left). Instead, they bought a used server rack for $100 and flush-mounted it in a custom-built alcove. They filled some of the space with rewired old laboratory equipment to give the rack a Dr. Strangelove-in-the-Batcave feel. Todd is particularly thrilled with the 1960s Hewlett-Packard oscilloscope (third unit from the top). Along an adjacent wall, they installed a flat-screen TV on a swing arm – their favorite DIY accomplishment.

The dining room table (left) is an old industrial table from an antique mall. The chairs are classic Emeco aluminum chairs from navy surplus. Mounted on the wall is a 1956 San Francisco bus destination sign that Todd found on eBay.

The kitchen and island counters are topped with Fireslate, a pressed concrete used in laboratories and kitchens. The 1950s factory stools are from a flea market. On the wall to the right of the counter is the flat-panel TV, which is like a digital picture frame. The TV is mounted on an Omnimount FP-CL swing arm so it can be pulled out to face the living room couch or the dining room table. The Omnimount was the most attractive and low-cost mounting arm they considered.

The light above the door to the bathroom (above) is from a navy shipyard. Hanging on the wall to the left of the doorway is an emergency lab kit from the Seton Source Book, a rich source, Todd says, of "everything an industrial fetishist could ever want." Additional industrial fixtures were purchased from McMaster-Carr. The kitchen cabinetry is from IKEA.

A 1970s galley cart from SAS airlines (left) has been transformed into a living-room bar. The pantry has a salvaged door (above left).

"Our Service for Ships means Ships for Service

The soap dish and shower shelf (above) are
aluminum utility-vehicle steps from **AW**
Direct. *"This is the best-designed soap dish
I've ever used,"* Todd says. *"Water drains away
cleanly, and the diamond plate holds the soap
in place and slightly elevated to dry."*

Todd stripped down the metal windowsills in
the bathroom and let them rust naturally.
An old San Francisco parking meter is mounted
on one of the sills.

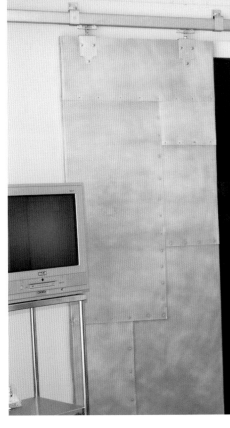

The bulletin board (opposite, top) and postings such as evacuation instructions are from decommissioned military bases throughout the Bay Area.

Upstairs in the master bedroom (above), Todd created dramatic sliding closet doors using aluminum sheets mounted in a collage pattern on wooden doors. The tracking system is from **McMaster-Carr.** *On the right is an aluminum cube locker from a navy ship. Todd stripped the locker, which now serves as a dresser.*

RESOURCES

AW DIRECT: awdirect.com

DEK-ING: dek-ing.com

EBAY: ebay.com

FIRESLATE: fireslate.com

IKEA: ikea.com

MCMASTER-CARR: mcmaster.com

NANA WALL SYSTEMS: nanawallsystems.com

OMNIMOUNT: omnimount.com

SETON: seton.ca

SHERWIN-WILLIAMS: sherwin-williams.com

photos by
costas voniatis

37.

turquoise's directional shift

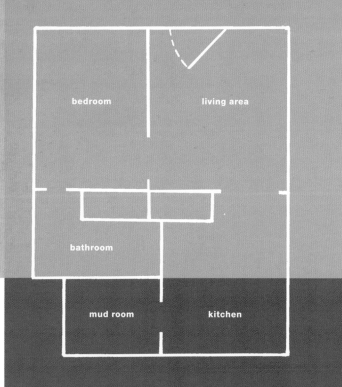

bedroom

living area

bathroom

mud room

kitchen

NAME: **VANESSA DE VARGAS (TURQUOISE)**

PROFESSION: **INTERIOR DESIGNER**

LOCATION: **VENICE BEACH, CALIFORNIA**

OWNED/RENTED: **OWNED**

SIZE: **500 SQUARE FEET**

TYPE: **1-BEDROOM BUNGALOW**

BUILT IN 1915

YEARS LIVED IN: **8**

(opposite, left) Turquoise created an entryway for her small bungalow by placing a console from IKEA *just inside the front door. The matching coral lamps are from* Urban Outfitters. *The vintage gold-painted mirror is from* Wertz Brothers. *The matching 1960s ottomans with steel bases came from an antiques store in Santa Barbara called the* Opportunity Shop.

...the colors and decorative details are so strong and dazzling that they distract you from what might be behind them.

About two years ago, the *New York Times* reported on a new style of interior design featuring a dark, grand, baroque look that Liberace would have loved. The *Times* called it "directional," and even though we didn't know what *directional* meant, the name has stuck. Vanessa de Vargas, aka Turquoise, is fully directional. Young, stylish, and good with a sewing machine, she is bringing back old-time luxury for pennies. You may be surprised that many of the touches are DIY, come from IKEA, or are cast-offs from someone else's home. Her approach is a little like decorating a stage set: the colors and decorative details are so strong and dazzling that they distract you from what might be behind them.

Turquoise is not alone. Los Angeles is the epicenter for directional style, which looks to the glamour and opulence of early Las Vegas and Hollywood and also takes cues from Latin culture. For inspiration, Turquoise also turns to Kelly Wearstler and to Jonathan Adler in New York. Central to her style, and what makes it so fresh and lively, is the strong, crisp movement from dark to light colors, which creates tremendous visual energy. Her bed looks particularly bright and scrumptious because it is held between warm, dark brown walls and bright white trim. In the living room, she puts a white table and lamp against a dark gray wall, making them pop. Creating contrast highlights the shapes, as well as the colors, of her nicest pieces.

For comparison, look at your own home. Are the walls linen white? Is the furniture beige and brown? Is the floor medium brown wood? Ours used to be, and Turquoise has been an influence. It is easy to live in the middle, away from the extremes, but it is far less interesting.

The mudroom, a study in 1970s style, contains a vintage Dorothy Draper *dresser (left) bought at a Beverly Hills estate sale, a shell chandelier from a Santa Barbara vintage store, reproduction Chinese flocked wallpaper from* Walnut Wallpaper, *and Lucite candleholders from an estate sale. Turquoise bought the frame above the dresser at* IKEA *and added the mirror.*

turquoise's
survey

Style

Modern/vintage eclectic.

Inspiration

Boutique hotels.

Favorite Elements

The crown molding and hardwood floors.

Biggest Challenge

Its small size, storage, and closet space.

What Friends Say

"It seems so much bigger than it is – it's
only 500 square feet?"

Biggest Embarrassment

You can hear everything that my
neighbors are saying and I am sure they
can hear me.

Proudest DIY

My IKEA TV cabinet, made to look like
a custom piece. I added molding and
Lucite handles and painted it black.

Biggest Indulgence

Paint and wallpaper.

Best Advice

Don't ever move, and I haven't!

Dream Sources

eBay, *Living Etc.*, *Domino* magazine,
ELLE Décor, *ELLE Decoration*, and
vintage home decorating books.
Woodson and Rummerfield's House of
Design, ModernOne, Jonathan Adler,
Weego Home, Barclay Butera.

*This mirror hangs above Turquoise's
custom-made bench just outside her
bathroom. She found it on* **eBay** *and it's
made by* **Honco**.

*The white tufted sofa
is from* **Wilton Cordrey**,
*which sells only to the
trade. The coffee table
is an ottoman with a
Lucite base purchased
from* **Jordan Cappella**. *The dark gray side walls are painted
in* **Behr's** *Amazon Stone, and the trim is high-gloss white.
Turquoise found the flocked gold-and-red wallpaper from the
1960s on* **eBay**. *The drapes and shag rug are from* **IKEA**.

The lacquered side tables with glass tops are empire style from the 1940s and came from Craigslist. *The 1960s black-smoked Lucite lamps are from* Karen Carson.

*Turquoise put floor-to-ceiling **IKEA** drapes behind her bed. To make them distinct from the off-the-shelf version, she attached black and silver trim with a Greek key design along the inside edges. Turquoise made the headboard using wood and dark gray velvet and attached it to wooden slats below the windowsill. The bedside tables are from eBay. She had them lacquered and added mirrored handles to the drawers. She customized hanging pendants from **IKEA** with black tassels from a notions store. The vintage Syroco wall clock and white birds are from **eBay**. The bedroom walls are painted in **Behr**'s Dark Granite.*

*Turquoise had the bench seat custom-made to fit this corner of her bedroom (left). She supplied the upholsterer with fabric from **Michael Levine**'s Fabric Store and then attached the legs and painted them white.*

*Turquoise found the 1950s chandelier (above, left) on **Craigslist**. The vases on the side tables are from **Umbra**. She painted them red. Turquoise's inspirations for her bedroom are boutique hotels in Los Angeles and Palm Springs. She wanted to create a space like a hotel bedroom "so I could pretend I was on vacation all the time."*

RESOURCES

BARCLAY BUTERA:

barclaybuterahome.com

BEHR: behr.com

BENJAMIN MOORE: benjaminmoore.com

COURTNEY'S ANTIQUES & VINTAGE:

310.451.3333

CRAIGSLIST: craigslist.org

DOMINO: dominomag.com

EBAY: ebay.com

ELLE DÉCOR: elledecor.com

IKEA: ikea.com

JONATHAN ADLER: jonathanadler.com

JORDAN CAPPELLA: jordancappella.com

KAREN CARSON: karencarson.com

KELLY WEARSTLER: kwid.com

LIVING ETC.: livingetc.com

MICHAEL LEVINE INC.: mlfabric.com

MODERNONE: modernone.1stdibs.com

OPPORTUNITY SHOP: 805.962.7233

SURFING COWBOYS: surfingcowboys.com

UMBRA: umbra.com

URBAN OUTFITTERS: urbanoutfitters.com

WALNUT WALLPAPER: walnutwallpaper.com

WEEGO HOME: weegohome.com

WERTZ BROTHERS: wertzbrothers.com

WILTON CORDREY: wiltoncordrey.com

WOODSON AND RUMMERFIELD'S

HOUSE OF DESIGN: wandrdesign.com

243

vanessa :: de vargas

Turquoise spruced up the original wood cabinets by painting them white and adding black trim. The dining table is a vintage Burke from Surfing Cowboys. The Louis XV–style chairs, from Courtney's in Santa Monica, are upholstered in black faux ostrich fabric with brass nail heads. The 1950s chandelier made of aluminum slats is from Craigslist, and the drapes are from IKEA. Framed with black molding is a vintage yellow bamboo wallpaper panel that Turquoise found on eBay. The walls are painted in Behr's Sparrow, and the floors are painted in Benjamin Moore black asphalt paint. Turquoise figured that if the asphalt paint worked on a street, it would be resilient enough for her kitchen floor.

photos by
jon leaver

38.
tyke and jon's topanga canyon casa

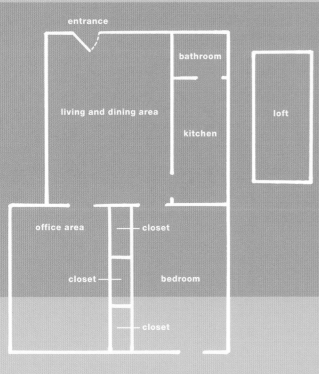

entrance

bathroom

living and dining area

loft

kitchen

office area — closet

closet — bedroom

closet

NAME: TYKE O'BRIEN AND JON LEAVER
PROFESSION: ENGLISH TEACHER (TYKE)
AND ART HISTORY PROFESSOR (JOHN)
LOCATION: TOPANGA CANYON,
CALIFORNIA
OWNED/RENTED: OWNED
SIZE: 1,200 SQUARE FEET
TYPE: SINGLE-FAMILY HOME
BUILT IN 1951
YEARS LIVED IN: 2

(opposite) The biggest room in Tyke and Jon's house is divided by low-lying IKEA *bookshelves into a living room and a dining area. The cowskin rug is from* Surfing Cowboys. *The laminate flooring is from* Hernandez Bros.

The IKEA *dining table is partnered with* Bellini *chairs from* Design Within Reach. *The vintage chandelier is from a swap meet. The pillow is by* Karl Erickson. *All of the pictures on the wall are by or from friends.*

Tyke and Jon's casa is fresh and bright, and it has a rock 'n' roll pedigree, having been a rehearsal studio for The Doors and The Eagles. Being fresh out of graduate school, Tyke and Jon have a limited budget but lots of passion. Both love design and consider it their major hobby. Their influences differ, however. Jon's parents are Welsh traditionalists; Tyke's mother is a "high modernist" and a "radical minimalist," who taught her the discipline of a budget. Together, they have a very pleasing synergy.

Tyke and Jon have updated the interior with bold color accents and an eclectic mix of twentieth-century design. The colors that stand out to us are in the bedroom and the living room, and provide two different examples of how accent color can be used. The bedroom is a simple stunner. As you enter, you are surrounded by a vibrant, rich green set off by two bright yellow lamps. Unlike the other rooms, these walls make the space smaller, creating a calm nighttime environment. In the living room, a pale sage accents the largest wall. Although it doesn't grab your attention like the green in the bedroom, it subtly highlights the peaked shape of the wall and the two-story height. It also adds warmth to the largest room in the house, which, if left unpainted, would seem cold and overwhelming.

Of particular note is Tyke and Jon's art collection, which makes a big impact. Every piece is a colorful curiosity and comes with a story about a friend or a store, or about having made it themselves. And there's a lot of art for a small home. They are also fortunate to have a yard, and what they have done offers some modest but ingenious ideas, such as using modern furniture in a rustic setting along with a simple awning held up with birch trees for a sweetly romantic solution.

Like many homes in this book, Tyke and Jon's points out the value of collecting over time. Their belongings have an accrued interest that far exceeds the two years they've lived in Topanga.

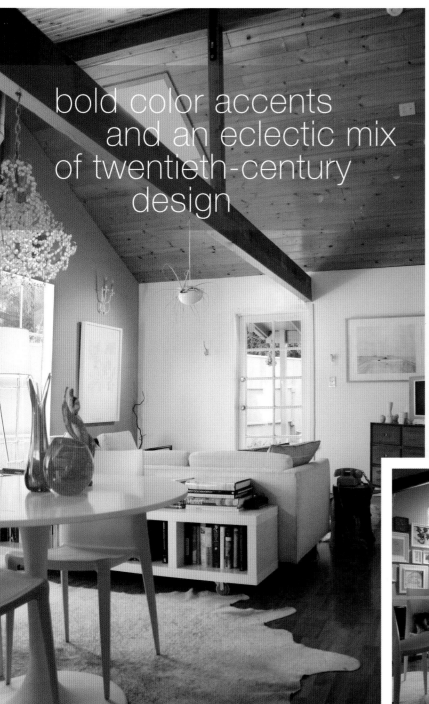

bold color accents and an eclectic mix of twentieth-century design

tyke and jon's
survey

Style
A hodgepodge of old and new with respect for the quirkiness and difficulty of the house itself.

Inspiration
Histories, happy accidents, and things we see in magazines, books, museums, traveling, and almost everywhere else.

Favorite Element
It's a tie between the big, open living room space with high pine-paneled ceilings and the nature surrounding the house, the huge pine trees, and the creek right alongside the house.

Biggest Challenge
Working within the budget and time constraints of two full-time educators.

What Friends Say
They like the house's history; it was the rehearsal studio for The Doors and – reputedly – The Eagles.

Biggest Embarrassment
The washer and dryer outside by the front door – but at least you can't see them from the street!

Proudest DIY
The teardown of a low ceiling covering two-thirds of the living/dining room. Now we can see the beautiful pine ceiling.

Biggest Indulgence
A beautiful French zinc bathtub from the 1800s, since we're not quite sure yet what to do with it! It's currently outside in true Topanga style.

Best Advice
No budget is too small. We began acquiring the things we love in this house when we were still in graduate school and renting an apartment, and we are still on a specific budget. Certain home improvement jobs need professionals, but we do whatever we can ourselves.

Dream Source
Arp on Third Street in West Hollywood. The housewares are all beautiful, especially anything by Ted Muehling.

A small sleeping loft overlooks the living room. The vintage sofa (left) is from the Rose Bowl Flea Market. The flokati rug is from Hidden Treasures. The walls are painted Ralph Lauren's Hopsack.

(opposite, left) Tyke and Jon reupholstered the vintage Danish chairs they purchased at Surfing Cowboys. The fabric and pillows are from Diamond Foam and Fabric. They often try their luck at the antique stores on the road from Palm Springs to Joshua Tree. At Pioneertown Antiques, they found the driftwood table.

(opposite, right) The Heywood-Wakefield dresser in the living room, which matches the nightstands in the bedroom, is from a swap meet. Many of the glass and ceramic objects were purchased at Jonathan Adler, OK, Zipper, and the LA MOCA Store.

Tyke and Jon renovated the dark kitchen (right) by adding a Corian counter from Home Depot. They repainting the lower cabinets with the highest gloss paint they could find (from Farrow and Ball) and put down semimatte black linoleum from RP Flooring. The faucet is from Delta. The walls are painted Ralph Lauren Sneaker White.

Tyke and Jon found the quilt in India and bought the lamps for $6 total at a **Salvation Army** store in Santa Barbara. The bed is from **IKEA**. The white shag rug is from **Hernandez Bros.**, and the white curtains are from **West Elm**. Tyke has had the small painting since childhood. The walls are Electric Avocado by **Behr**.

Tyke and Jon found the yellow chair in an alley and used it as the element around which to design the entire bedroom. The yellow faux bamboo table in the nook is from the **Salvation Army**.

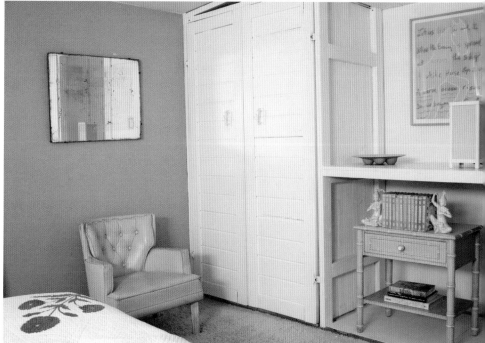

RESOURCES

ARP: 323.653.7764

BEHR: behr.com

DELTA: deltafaucet.com

DESIGN WITHIN REACH: dwr.com

DIAMOND FOAM AND FABRIC: 323.931.3626

FARROW AND BALL: farrow-ball.com

HERNANDEZ BROS.:

hernandezwholesaleflooring.com

HEYWOOD-WAKEFIELD:

heywood-wakefield.com

HIDDEN TREASURES:

hiddentreasuresla.com

HOME DEPOT: homedepot.com

IKEA: ikea.com

JONATHAN ADLER: jonathanadler.com

KARTELL: kartell.it

LA MOCA STORE: moca-la.org

OK: okstore.la

RALPH LAUREN: rlhome.polo.com

ROSE BOWL FLEA MARKET: rgcshows.com

RP FLOORING: 818.888.3938

SALVATION ARMY: salvationarmyusa.org

SURFING COWBOYS: surfingcowboys.com

TED MUEHLING: tedmuehling.com

WEST ELM: westelm.com

ZIPPER: zippergifts.com

*The **Eames** recliner, sideboard, and desk in the office are from various antique stores and swap meets. The Feruccio Laviani lamp is from **Kartell**, and the shelves are from **IKEA**.*

photos by
angie cao

39.
victoria's
bomo pad

dining area

living area

kitchen

bathroom

closet

bedroom

NAME: VICTORIA SMITH

PROFESSION: COMMERCIAL ART BUYER

LOCATION: PACIFIC HEIGHTS,
SAN FRANCISCO

OWNED/RENTED: RENTED

SIZE: 800 SQUARE FEET

TYPE: 1-BEDROOM IN AN 8-UNIT
VICTORIAN BUILDING

YEARS LIVED IN: 1

She is more obsessive than most about putting her stamp on everything she brings into her home.

Before we met Victoria, she had coined her own style, BoMo, for Bohemian Vintage-Modern, which is on display in her awesome Bay Area home.

Typically indefatigable and intrepid, Victoria never tires of hunting down treasures. To keep track of her sources of inspiration, she has a journal of design ideas. Whenever she wants to try something new, she opens her journal. When asked where her inspiration comes from, Victoria can't be pinned down. She credits talented friends and coworkers, San Francisco history, art, thought-provoking novels, and great fashion. She weaves together these eclectic threads in an apartment that has a unique history. It was the home of the late Herb Caen, the legendary columnist.

Uniqueness is a priority for Victoria, and she is a bit more obsessive than most about putting her stamp on everything she brings into her home. Even if the original object is shiny and new, she personalizes its surroundings to counteract any mass-produced banality. "If you're going to have a Pottery Barn–type sofa," she says, "you have to mix it with unusual and eclectic items to bring individuality to the room."

As you enter Victoria's apartment, notice how organized and comfortable it seems without feeling the least bit "done." Hers is a lived-in style. All the little pockets of collections invite you to be curious and look close. Putting together rooms that have a strong sense of composition right down to the details is one of the special qualities here.

The art deco buffet (left) in the dining room, her favorite DIY, has been with Victoria throughout her adult life. She stripped and refinished it herself. The black and white pottery is from eBay *and* Cost Plus. *Victoria uses the chalkboard to display menus for her guests or to write shopping lists.*

The 1960s Lane sideboard/cabinet (right) is from the Alameda Flea Market. *The framed pictures are part of a large collection of photos of family and friends.*

...rooms that have a
strong sense of
composition right down
to the details...

victoria's
survey

Style

My style is Bohemian Vintage-Modern.
Very eclectic, with modernist pieces
thrown in.

Inspiration

I see inspiration everywhere. That's why
the apartment ends up being so eclectic.
It's difficult for me to stay completely
loyal to just one style. I get a lot of inspiration from the flea market, magazines
like *Domino* and *ELLE Décor*, San Francisco boutiques like Swallowtail and Nest,
and stores like Design Within Reach.

Favorite Element

I love the light – the bay window and
French doors to the terrace bring tons of
sunshine streaming in all day long.

Biggest Challenge

It's a rental, so I can't do too much.
At first the stained glass windows in the
bedroom seemed like a real challenge
to decorate around. They're huge and
they're not really my taste, since I lean
more toward modernism. But I learned
to embrace them and created a kind
of Moroccan theme with bright pillows
and artwork to accent the window
colors, and now I quite like it.

What Friends Say

My friends seem to feel very comfortable at my house; they come early and
stay late. A lot of them ask me for design
advice. They usually say it's like a
museum. They like to look around and
take in all my collections.

Biggest Embarrassment

I hate the hideous kitchen tile. It's retro
seventies, but not in a cool way. It's an
ugly brown, mottled, flower motif. The
kitchen floor is black linoleum that is
really difficult to keep clean with a hairy
Labrador in the house.

Proudest DIY

I purchased my art deco buffet at a
yard sale for $5, stripped it, and sanded
it down to its natural finish. It has been
in every one of my apartments for the
past twenty years.

Biggest Indulgence

The bed linens.

Best Advice

Reading Maxwell Gillingham-Ryan's first
book taught me a lot about editing out
the things I don't need and traveling light.
It's hard for me to get rid of things. I wish
I could be minimalist, but I know I can't,
so I'm streamlining a lot.

Dream Source

If I could buy a ton of McCobb and
Eames originals, I'd be pretty happy.
Some beautiful original artwork would be
nice as well. I also like throwing in the
odd piece from Anthropologie Home.

Victoria's sitting area in the bay window takes advantage of the copious natural light. The 1960s chair and ottoman (above) are from **Craigslist**. The owner had kept them enclosed in plastic slipcovers, so they were in perfect condition. The table is midcentury modern from **Apartment**. The magazine rack comes from the **Container Store**. Victoria likes the paper lanterns from **Crate & Barrel**, **IKEA**, and **Cost Plus** because they give off a great soft light.

Victoria found the two midcentury leatherette chairs and the flokati rug (left) on **Craigslist**. The copper fireplace surround and Rico Suave portrait are from the **Alameda Flea Market**. She found the floor-to-ceiling black pole lamp on **eBay**.

The pass-through window (below) connects the kitchen and the dining room. The rattan chair is a midcentury knockoff from Pier 1, *and the bench is a* George Nelson *knockoff from* Urban Outfitters. *The clock is from the* Crate & Barrel Outlet. *To create some of the art on the walls, Victoria scanned old photographs, enlarged them, and printed them on an inkjet printer. Her parents bought the painting of a San Francisco cable car by* Flavia *at a parking-lot art show in the 1960s. Her father gave it to her when she moved to San Francisco.*

(opposite, top left) Victoria's lounge/inspiration area is in a corner of the bedroom. Over the IKEA *sleeper couch, she mounted a tension wire from* West Elm *that comes with clips for hanging notes and mementos. The coffee table is a vintage cart from* Russian Hill Antiques. *The glass allows the rusted top to show through.*

(opposite, top right) The great wall unit belonged to a Russian record collector. Victoria bought it from him on Craigslist. *The table is an* IKEA *Docksta, a* Saarinen *knockoff. She wanted more space in the dining room, so she chose a small table. The* Mies van der Rohe *chairs are from* Craigslist. *The Venetian glass chandelier belonged to the previous tenants. Victoria loved the chandelier, and they offered to leave it for her in exchange for cleaning the apartment after they moved to France.*

(above and opposite, bottom) The bold stained glass windows initially were Victoria's biggest design challenge. She now views them as comfy and inviting. She chose an understated Malm birch-finish platform bed from IKEA.

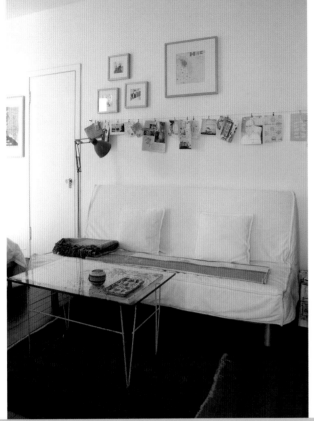

RESOURCES

ALAMEDA FLEA MARKET: antiquesbybay.com

ANTHROPOLOGIE HOME: anthropologie.com

APARTMENT: 415.255.1100

CONTAINER STORE: containerstore.com

COST PLUS: worldmarket.com

CRAIGSLIST: craigslist.org

CRATE & BARREL OUTLET: crateandbarrel.com

EBAY: ebay.com

ELLE DÉCOR: elledecor.com

IKEA: ikea.com

NEST: 415.292.6199

PIER 1 IMPORTS: pier1.com

RUSSIAN HILL ANTIQUES: 415.441.5561

SWALLOWTAIL: swallowtailsf.com

URBAN OUTFITTERS: urbanoutfitters.com

WEST ELM: westelm.com

photos by
jill slater

40.

yoktan's tenement of the found

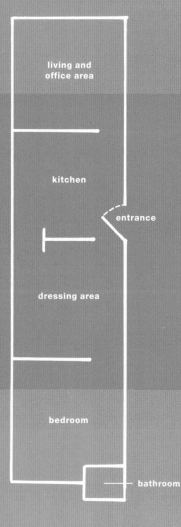

living and office area

kitchen

entrance

dressing area

bedroom

bathroom

NAME: YOKTAN HADDAD
PROFESSION: OWNER OF A WEB DESIGN COMPANY AND WRITER
LOCATION: EAST VILLAGE, NYC
OWNED/RENTED: OWNED
SIZE: 400 SQUARE FEET
TYPE: 4-ROOM APARTMENT IN AN 1880s 4-STORY WALK-UP
YEARS LIVED IN: 1.5

...he has learned
that limitations can
unlock creativity.

Yoktan is the epitome of the artistic DIY spirit that thrives in the urban environment. He proves that it doesn't take money to have style; it takes patience and imagination. "I like to convert things," says Yoktan. Everything in his apartment has been acquired rather than bought and often does double duty as both art object and functional furniture. His ability to see beauty in unusual finds is inspirational.

Yoktan brings a discerning curatorial eye to his salvage decor. Everything is carefully considered, and nothing feels random or accidental. When he discovers an object, he might integrate it immediately or he might wait patiently before deciding on just the right place to showcase it. For example, he came across some 1940s ice trays but is not yet sure how he wants to transform them. When he found a piece of Formica-covered plywood, he quickly saw he could use it to transform his ladder into a coffee table.

He is almost empathetic about objects, feeling that he *must* save them from the landfill and obscurity. Yet his collections have themes: he is drawn to refrigerators, creative storage alternatives, and things with a '60s palette.

Like many curbside shoppers, flea market aficionados, and Dumpster divers, Yoktan formed his habit not from choice, but from necessity. Now that he can afford to shop, it pains him to succumb to the occasional store-bought item. Why? Because he has learned that limitations can unlock creativity. Yoktan's home is a work in progress, and given his patience and skill, he will continue to transform it over the coming years.

Yoktan keeps all his tools in the living room in a cabinet (above) made of four card catalog drawers. The front room (right) receives the most natural light and is used as both office and living room. The red couch was found on the street, as were the glass and metal bookshelves on the far wall.

yoktan's
survey

Style

Street refashioning, garbage salvation, and object re-adaptation.

Inspiration

Finding or inheriting something and figuring out what to do with it and preferably using it for something other than its original purpose.

Favorite Elements

The elaborate wooden frames around windows and doors and the high quality of building materials and skill that went into this apartment even though it was built as a tenement.

Biggest Challenge

Adapting to, versus redesigning, existing elements of the apartment.

What Friends Say

It's a museum, I'm maniacal, and I should take up interior design as a career.

Biggest Embarrassment

You can hear everything that is happening in the toilet when you are in the bedroom; it's embarrassing when someone is sleeping over.

Proudest DIY

The stepladder converted into a coffee table.

Biggest Indulgence

Exposing all the brick walls and having them repainted.

Best Advice

Don't put bars or gates over the windows.

Dream Sources

NYC streets; garbage is just a lack of imagination.

The console (top) is a street find. Yoktan kept it because of its color. It works as a striking gallery for his orange-themed novelties. Yoktan continues to need the ladder (above) for paint removal and wood stripping. When it is not in use, he converts it into a coffee table with a found piece of Formica held in place with heavy-duty clamps.

Near the kitchen sink, Yoktan installed
an old medicine cabinet (above left) and
attached a silver spoon as a handle.

Yoktan removed a century's worth of
paint from the wooden boards that make
up the kitchen backsplash (above right).
As in many old tenements, the bathtub
is in the kitchen. He covers it with a
piece of wood to create a work surface for
preparing meals. The first shelf of the
cabinet has a dish organizer fashioned
from red plastic Coke bottle carriers.

To the right of the medicine cabinet
is a butter tray (right) from a 1950s
refrigerator, used to hold toothpaste and
razor. The spring still works and keeps
the lid shut.

(opposite) Exposed shelving holds kitchen supplies as well as vintage cans and bottles. The kitchen wall displays '50s, '60s, and '70s freezer doors that Yoktan has collected over the years.

Old valises and a found midcentury dresser (right) make an attractive display as well as provide storage. Two refrigerator crispers — one on top of the valises, the other under the straw hat — contain clothing.

Each room in Yoktan's apartment is ten by ten feet. The four rooms are arranged one after another off a hallway that runs forty feet along one side of the apartment. The only piece of furniture in the bedroom (below) is a futon on wooden shipping pallets.

RESOURCES

IKEA: ikea.com

home categories . . .

To find a home like yours, or to simply browse according to these broad distinguishing traits, flip to the table of CONTENTS (page 6) to find the page on which each house tour starts.

GEOGRAPHY

east

Alison's Design to the Max

Alton and André's Deco Light in Chelsea

Bri and Chad's Fab on a Budget

Charles and Julie's Perfect Garden Apartment

Curtis's Paint by Numbers

Dante's Industriousness

Dixie's Vintage Carnival

Gideon and Tracy's Pocket Knife

Hakarl and Jili's Bold Bright Moves

Ivar's Pared Down and Simple

James and Margaret's Iconic Studio

Jane and Darko's Cozy Thicket

Jenny and Clove's LA-ish Studio

Jill's DIY Laboratory

Justine and David's Home Away from Home

Marlon's Blue Pad

Michael and Corrie's Mini Mansion

Patrick's Cosmo-Urban Studio Rental

Paul's Pivoting Perfection

Raelene and Jose's Miami Vice

Robert's Mitchell-Lama Labor of Love

Sara Kate and Maxwell's Gourmet Shoe Box

Yoktan's Tenement of the Found

midwest

Andreas's Greektown Loft

Dana's Sunny Logan Square Apartment

David's Andersonville Apartment

Jessica and Andrius, Artists in Residence

Joseph's Wicker Nest

Marilyn and Peter's Home Studio

Melissa and Matt's Design Lab

Shannon and Emmett's From Factory to Family

west

David and Im's OneSpace

Gregory and Emily's Silverlake Sanctuary

Jonathan's '60s Retro

Shauna and Fred's More Dash than Cash

Thom's San Fran Delight

Todd and Nicole's Project Precita

Turquoise's Directional Shift

Tyke and Jon's Topanga Canyon Casa

Victoria's BoMo Pad

an index of sorts.

continued

Apartment Therapy Since its launch in 2004, ApartmentTherapy.com has become the largest and most influential design blog on the Web for those interested in creating a beautiful, organized, and healthy home. Its network of regional and subject blogs share over one million unique visitors a month and have received accolades from the *New York Times*, the *Wall Street Journal*, *Domino* magazine, and *Newsweek* among others.

Maxwell Gillingham-Ryan

"One part interior designer, one part life coach," Maxwell is the founder of ApartmentTherapy.com. He's a regular commentator on the HGTV show *Small Space, Big Style* and has been featured in the *New York Times*, the *New York Post*, the *New York Observer*, and the *Wall Street Journal*. He lives in a 250-square foot apartment in New York's West Village with his wife, Sara-Kate, a food writer.

Jill Slater

All around "urbanista," Jill has spent her life embellishing on life's template—through art, craft, travel, photography, dance, fashion, the written word, and design. As the Inside Out house tour columnist for Apartment Therapy.com, she is privy to a wide and varied swath of New York homes. Jill lives in Lower Manhattan in a miniloft that she designed and built from the inside out.

Janel Laban

ApartmentTherapy.com managing editor Janel has the distinction of having lived in (and decorated) apartments in every Apartment Therapy city over the last 20 years. She graduated with a degree in fine arts from the School of Visual Arts in New York City. Janel now lives in Chicago with her husband and son in a small but loved apartment in Lincoln Park.